*The Ministry of
Pastoral Counseling*

THE MINISTRY OF PASTORAL COUNSELING

James D. Hamilton

BAKER BOOK HOUSE
Grand Rapids, Michigan

584945

Copyright 1972 by Beacon Hill Press
Reprinted 1972 by Baker Book House
ISBN: 0-8010-4069-8
Printed in the United States of America

Seventh printing, March 1983

Quotations from *The New Testament in Modern English,* © J. B. Phillips, 1958. Used by permission of the Macmillan Co.

To
DOROTHY

Contents

Preface

This book is written as an elementary guide for the minister who has had little education and experience in pastoral counseling. Its purpose is twofold: (1) to examine the basic elements of counseling and (2) to show the place of counseling in the pastoral ministry.

Acknowledgments

Appreciation is expressed to my wife, Dorothy, and to Betty B. Robertson for typing the manuscript, and to Philip E. Reed for offering valuable criticism and evaluation of the material in this book.

—J. D. H.

1

The Nature of Pastoral Counseling

The contemporary minister is afforded many opportunities for engaging in a wide range of counseling activities in his parish. He is called upon for counsel by persons of all ages troubled by many and varied problems. No minister can avoid counseling unless he locks himself in his study.[1] His responsibility is often to a large group of people who come from various backgrounds and who are grappling with emotionally disturbing difficulties of many descriptions.

A pastor is not a psychologist, yet he is called upon for psychological counseling. He is not a vocational counselor, but he is sought for help in this area. He is not an educational counselor, but often youth come to him with problems concerning their courses of study. Neither is he a psychiatrist; nevertheless he is sometimes confronted with the deep-seated problems of persons needing psychiatric care and must, therefore, be aware of the manifestations of these problems in order to make intelligent referrals. However, he must above all else, know how to counsel persons with religious problems, and so should become as proficient in this area as possible.

THE NEED FOR PASTORAL COUNSELING

This is a complex age. It is an age of crisis and tension, one in which industrialization and mechanization pull individuals into its wake, confronting them with problems of varying degree and magnitude.[2] Forced choices are the rule rather than the exception and these choices carry deep interpersonal implications. Modern man cannot be an isolate. This means that his actions and reactions, more than at any other time in history, affect the actions and reactions of his fellows. Great numbers of people staggered by "life" and its multiplicity of problems, feel the need for help and counsel. Certainly not all of these troubled people will seek the advice of a minister, but many of them will.[3] Therefore it is necessary that the pastor be a competent counselor who can serve the needs of persons who come to him for help with their problems.

Pastoral counseling is as old as the ministry.[4] Holman says:

> The cure of souls—the spiritual care of members of a congregation—is an ancient function of the Christian church and the Christian clergyman. Perhaps the most fundamental aspect of the minister's task has always been his work with individuals. In intimate personal contact with his people, the pastor has sought to bring help to the tempted, spiritual renewal to the defeated, assurance of forgiveness to the penitent, comfort to the troubled, guidance to the perplexed, courage to the sick and bereaved, and in a multitude of ways has sought to meet the peculiarly personal needs of the individuals who comprise his congregation.[5]

It has always been the task of ministers to function as mediators between men and their problems. Wood says that it is not a matter of whether a minister shall counsel but how well. He reported that 87 percent of laymen believe that skill in counseling ought to be a part of the training of a minister.[6]

What Pastoral Counseling Is

Pastoral counseling differs from other counseling in one major respect, namely, the inclusion of the religious dimension. "The goal of spiritual counseling is to bring men and women into right relationship with God and to lead them into the abundant life."[7] "To save" in the Greek means to heal or make whole; therefore salvation is wholeness, soundness, deliverance from everything that blights and warps human personality and prevents fellowship with God.

The element of change in our society has implications for pastoral counseling. Change is not a new phenomenon; it has always been present. Philosophers for centuries have been asking, "What, amid all change, does not change?" The answer, "Nothing." Heraclitus, centuries ago, said, "One cannot step into the same river twice." By this statement he affirmed the age-old condition of change. All past societies have had to cope with change but ours is undergoing more rapid, complex changes than others before it. Goldstein points out that those in places of social leadership will be instrumental in affecting the forms of adaptation that society will take in coping with that change.[8] This means that the pastor-counselor who serves in a social-leadership role must be equipped to serve his church families as a wise counselor under the complicated conditions caused by rapid change. Hulme says, "The characteristics of our age that drive people into the protective darkness of isolation also create the emotional disturbance that causes them to need counseling."[9]

Many persons facing this complex world are plagued with an inadequacy to cope with the problems arising out of it. Persons with religious orientations will usually go to their ministers for guidance and help. Thus it becomes the task of the minister to help them form a healthy and adequate attitude and approach toward life. There needs to be developed within them the human strength which, combined with divine resources, will prepare them to meet the demands of a highly complex world. This means, then, that the function of the counseling relationship will be twofold: (1) "to strengthen the ego, or the self, or the conscious functions of a person through which the integrative, maturing processes are achieved" (the human dimension), and (2) to appropriate the spiritual resources that God offers (the divine dimension).[10]

The pastor-counselor must remember that the emotional injuries that have been inflicted upon individuals have come through faulty relationships with emotionally significant persons.[11] These injuries may be healed by some other person who, too, is emotionally significant. In many cases this will be the pastor who will help those hurt individuals by his counseling ministry. "Oftentimes the people who come to consult a minister have lost faith in themselves as well as in God and their fellow-men."[12] The minister must help to rebuild those confidences so that a clearer outlook may be achieved.

Pastoral counseling and psychiatry are similar but not synonymous. Psychiatry, though not necessarily opposed to the religious aspect, does not depend upon it either for its diagnosis or its therapy. Pastoral counseling, on the other hand, is based fundamentally upon the religious outlook and interpretation. It consciously attempts to develop in individuals a relationship with God which gives access to the spiritual resources that flow from Him. Bonnell characterizes the pastor-counselor's task as follows:

> The minister who brings men and women into a vital contact with God, who teaches them how to use the Bible for spiritual development, how to meditate, how to pray, how to develop a strong and radiant faith, will be rendering an invaluable service to the minds and bodies of his parishioners as well as to their souls.[13]

A true counseling situation does not necessarily exist when a pastor and a parishioner are engaged in conversation together. Counseling is not the mere exchange of words. A need must be known by the counselee and he must see the need of receiving assistance in solving the problem that is troubling him. Hiltner says:

> A true counseling situation exists when a parishioner recognizes that something is wrong, senses that this is in some measure within him, and is convinced that a professional person may be able to help him with it, not by giving him the answer but by aiding him to clarify it for himself. [14]

Thus, counseling is an interpersonal relationship in which the pastor and the parishioner concentrate on clarifying the feelings and problems of the latter and both understand that this is what they are endeavoring to accomplish. It will be necessary for the minister to aid his counselee in overcoming his inner conflicts and tensions by helping him to verbalize his problems so that they can be critically examined. When this is achieved, the true counseling relationship exists.

PERSONAL QUALIFICATIONS

Stolz says, "The personality of the pastor himself is of primary importance in his work. A mature and wholesome outlook on life is essential to good pastoral service." [15] He indicates that when the blind attempt to lead the blind the outcome is disastrous to both.

The more emotionally mature the pastor is, the greater will be his faculty for understanding and accepting what his parishioners express to him. If he is not staggered by life himself, and is able to communicate his mature and wholesome outlook to his people, he will find that they will seek him for aid in resolving their problems. Bonnell said that no clergyman can adequately minister to the deepest needs in human hearts who has not learned to deal effectively with his own. [16] In a sense, a mark of his own adjustment will be his ability to draw his people to himself. This will be accomplished by his very life, not merely by inviting his people to come to him with their needs. "A person cannot communicate the deep, intimate aspects of his life to another unless he has a feeling of security, confidence and trust in the other."[17] This is absolutely essential if sound counseling is to be done. People will come to the pastor for counseling only if they trust him and see in him the maturity they desire for themselves.

Of prime importance in evaluating the personal qualities of a pastor is a consideration of his ability to understand himself—his attitudes, motives, and disposition. Socrates' dictum was, "Know thyself." This should be the goal of each pastor. Without this self-knowledge other qualities and capabilities in the pastor are of little value. Hiltner says:

> Learning about the parishioner, his immense verities and unique individualities, is of great importance. But we may know all about the parishioners and still be unable to enter into a fruitful counseling relationship. . . . I have come to feel that learning about our own attitudes in counseling is the most subtle but most important aspect of our task.[18]

Philosophy and Values in Counseling

In 1955, Cribbin[19] made an exhaustive study of over 200 texts and journal articles to learn the place of philosophy and values in counseling. Following is a summary of the philosophical principles he discovered in his research:

1. Counseling is based on the recognition of the dignity and worth of the individual and on his right to personal assistance in time of need.

2. Counseling is client-centered, being concerned with the optimum development of the whole person and the fullest realization of his potentialities for individual and social ends.

3. Counseling is a continuous, sequential, and educational process.

4. Counseling has a responsibility to society as well as to the individual.

5. Counseling must respect the right of every person to accept or refuse the help and services it offers.

6. Counseling is oriented around cooperation, not compulsion.

7. Counseling implies assistance given persons in making wise choices, plans, interpretations, and adjustments in the critical situations of life.

8. Counseling demands a comprehensive study of the individual in his cultural setting by use of every scientific technique available.

9. Counseling should be entrusted only to those who are naturally endowed for the task and have the necessary training and experience.

10. The focus of counseling is on helping the individual realize and actualize his best self rather than on solving problems, whether they are problems of the individual or those of the school or other institutions.

11. Counseling must be under constant scientific evaluation in terms of its effectiveness.

Counseling for Change

The ultimate goal of counseling is to effect change in the counselee. Following are some specific aspects of change the pastor seeks to help his parishioner achieve:

1. *A reduction of anxiety.* This enables the person to redirect his energy toward a resolution of the immediate problem rather than using it to feed his anxiety.

2. *An achievement of greater objectivity.* Counseling serves to dilute the counselee's subjectivity by bringing objectivity through clarification of the problem and an understanding of the counselee's relationship to it.

3. *An advancement in motivation.* This results when one begins to see that there is a basis for real hope that his problem can be solved.

4. *An ability to reality-test emotional states.* This is achieved when one learns the *why* behind the *what* that is troubling him.

5. *An increasing ability to evaluate and confront guilt.* This results when one learns to test the validity of his guilt (not all guilt feelings are valid) and then deal with it constructively in both the human and the divine dimensions.

6. *A growing self-concept.* This is achieved by effecting a closer relationship between self-perceptions and self-experiences.

7. *An increased skill in interpersonal relationships.* This is effected in two ways: (1) in experiencing openness with the pastor in the counseling relationship and (2) by experiencing openness with others in life situations.

8. *An increasing ability to work, to love, and to be.* These results are obtained when the person learns to redirect his energy and interests from a crippling subjectivity toward a liberating objectivity.

9. *A growing confidence in facing the future.* This results when one has experienced the "sweet taste of victory" in dealing with a serious problem, thus giving him the belief that he can, by God's help, solve problems that will arise in the future.

10. *An enlarging concept of God and a better understanding of His loving nature.* These result when a pastor aids his parishioner to truly accept the God of the Bible rather than a view of God based on one's feelings.

11. *A growing Christlikeness in attitude and behavior.* This is achieved when one learns to practice the precepts of our Lord in both the intra-personal and interpersonal dimensions.

12. *A growing ability to express Christian faith in service.* This is effected by learning to understand that we are saved to serve.

2

The Boundaries of Pastoral Counseling

INTRODUCTION

Counseling is both quite old and quite new. It is old in the sense that there have always been mediators between men and their problems. That is, there have always been persons who have served in the role of counselor to persons facing problems in their lives. Sometimes these counselors were self-appointed. Sometimes they were appointed by others by virtue of their position or age, such as seers, sages, wise men, or prophets. This was particularly so in the Oriental world. As one studies Bible history he can see how prominent a place was given to the role of the counselor in Jewish life and thought. The Old Testament, particularly the Book of Proverbs, has many references to counseling. Historically, counseling has been viewed more as a function rather than as a profession. That is, counseling was a kind of by-product of another role or profession.

Counseling is new in the sense that, as a separate professional discipline, it actually came of age only early in this century. It is historically linked to three things: (1) the emergence of trait and factor psychology; (2) the development of motivational psychology; and (3) the rise of vocational guidance, which dates back to the publication of a book by Frank Parson entitled *Choosing a Vocation*. The modern counseling movement began when his book was published early in this century.

There has been a continuing shift in emphasis from problems to persons in the counseling movement. Thus the goal has come to be the life adjustment of the individual. It is believed that it is the person who needs help rather than a problem which needs to be solved.

Counseling means many things to many people. Actually the term "counselor" is a very abused word. It is not uncommon to discover that there are persons who serve as loan counselors, camp counselors, fashion counselors, or even lawn counselors. Certainly these are careless uses for a good word.

Advising, Counseling, and Psychotherapy

Pastoral counseling ranges between the two extremes of advising and deep psychotherapy. Pastoral counseling is not advising, because advising aims primarily at solving surface problems. Neither can it be said that pastoral counseling is deep psychotherapy, for this aims at making major changes in behavior through major changes in the structure of the personality. Between these two extremes of advising and deep psychotherapy the work of pastoral counseling is done. Pastoral counseling can be characterized by the following:

1. It is a spiritual-psychological interaction between pastor and parishioner, the methods and purpose of which, as

noted above, range between the two extremes of advising and deep psychotherapy.

2. The recipients of counseling are called counselees or parishioners.

3. Counseling is done with persons who are believed to be normal.

4. Counseling is done with normal people who are often frustrated.

5. It aims at self-understanding in the light of the person's potential and it requires modification of attitudes and behavior.

6. More emphasis is given to the present and the conscious than to the past and the unconscious.

7. It is done within the Christian context and its goals are thoroughly Christian.

Inasmuch as the boundaries of pastoral counseling are determined by these seven characteristics, it is important that they be examined more closely. In doing so it can be learned what pastoral counseling is and how it differs from other methods of helping persons. This will provide for us the boundaries within which it operates.

1. Pastoral counseling is a spiritual-psychological interaction between a pastor and a parishioner for the purpose of resolving the difficulty of the latter. This may range all the way from difficulty in coping with life in general to difficulty in coping with some problem in particular. This spiritual-psychological encounter may be formalized; that is, it may be prearranged with a definite time and place set for the counseling situation. However, it may be informal; that is, a helping relationship may be established with the parishioner when a pastor is in contact with him in some other type of relationship and the counseling situation emerges out of it. It may be initiated simply by a parishioner saying, "By the way, Pastor, there is something that has been troubling me and I would like to talk with you about it." It does not matter how the helping contact is established; that is, whether it is formal

23

or informal. The essential thing is that each is aware of his role in the relationship.

This spiritual-psychological interaction may entail multiple sessions or it may require only one session. The wise pastor knows that serious problems will not likely be solved in a single session. Therefore he will help his parishioner see the need for continued counseling until the problem is adequately resolved. This is not to say that great problems cannot be solved in a single session. However, in most cases this will not happen. Both pastor and parishioner will hope for, but not expect, quick solutions.

As has been said, spiritual-psychological interaction will neither be advising nor deep psychotherapy. Advising is usually done with a minimum of interpersonal encounter. It is largely one-directional, from the person giving help to the person receiving help. Thus, it ignores the value of deep interpersonal interaction. This interaction is vital to the ongoing of a valid, helping relationship. Deep psychotherapy aims at making major changes in the individual through a long and arduous restructuring of the personality. Only persons with extensive training, great skill, and much experience are qualified to do this kind of therapy. Most pastors are not qualified in this manner.

2. The recipients of pastoral counseling are called counselees or parishioners. Persons who seek help from a professional counselor or psychologist are usually called clients. Persons who go to psychiatrists for help are usually referred to as patients. While these distinctions may not appear to be important, in actuality they are. A client is one who employs the services of a professional person and usually pays a fee for those services. The term "patient" places the helping relationship in a medical frame of reference. Inasmuch as the pastor is neither a paid professional counselor nor a medical man, it is not appropriate to call his parishioners clients or patients.

3. Pastoral counseling is done with normal people. The

term "normal," as it relates to personality, is most difficult to define. Some would say that it is impossible to define. Others would deny that a truly normal person exists. This belief arises out of the commonly held theory that the difference between mental health and mental illness is not a difference in kind but a difference in degree. This theory holds, then, that there is a measure of illness in the mentally healthy person and a measure of health in the mentally ill person. One psychiatrist, when asked to describe a normal person, is reported to have said, "I can't. I have never met one." All of this notwithstanding, this book asserts that normal persons *do* exist.

Without attempting to properly define normalcy, an attempt will be made here to describe it. A normal person is one who has enough contact with reality to do a reasonably adequate job of coping with the major aspects of his life. He can work, play, eat, sleep, study, drive, and converse in such a manner as to keep his life together. While he may sometimes be frustrated, he is not disintegrated. He is not viewed by his associates as strange, odd, or dangerous. The pastor can help "normal" people as they confront problems in their lives. However, he cannot be of much immediate and direct help to "abnormal" people. These are people who have lost, or are losing, contact with reality, who are engaging in bizarre behavior, and who are dangerous to themselves and to others. These persons need to be referred to either a clinical psychologist or a psychiatrist.

4. Pastoral counseling is done with normal people who are frustrated. Frustration is the blocking or interference of a need or goal through some barrier or obstruction. Frustration is both frequent and inevitable. An unfrustrated life is inconceivable, for the basic needs of man are often unmet and his goals are often blocked. Therefore frustration will be present in varying degree in every person. It is not a question of *if* frustration will occur; rather, it is a question of *how much* there will be. Frustration creates great emotional pain and

causes one to lose his objectivity. He gets lost in his problem. He does not see a clear way out of it; therefore he seeks help. Frustration is present to a rather large degree in most of the persons who seek counseling from their pastors.

5. Pastoral counseling aims at self-understanding in the light of the person's potential and it requires a modification of both attitude and behavior. Attitudes and behavior are the two major areas in which the pastor works.

6. In pastoral counseling more emphasis is given to the present and conscious than to the past and unconscious. In this respect, pastoral counseling differs markedly from psychoanalysis. Psychoanalysis deals to a great extent with both a person's past experiences and his unconscious drives. It believes that a person can be understood only in terms of his past and that one's conscious thinking and behavior are determined by unconscious forces. The pastor does not have the training, skill, and experience to do this kind of work. That is the reason why he must center his emphasis upon the present and upon the conscious. These are the two dimensions that are immediately avilable to him and these are the two areas in which he is qualified to work.

7. Pastoral counseling is done within the Christian context and its goals are thoroughly Christian in nature. The pastor is not, and should not be, a secular counselor. While there may not be enough secular counselors to meet the needs of persons in this complex society, it is not the task of pastors to fill up that void. Pastors have their own unique domain in which to work. That domain is within the framework of the Christian tradition and Christian theology.

The pastor-counselor is aware that his counseling must have a divine dimension. He is deeply aware that man is a spiritual being whose spiritual needs can be met only by God. The pastor-counselor views man in relationship to God and he sees man in terms of eternal values. He seeks to bring man into right relationship with God. The pastor has one primary goal in mind—that his parishioner, through counseling, will be brought to a greater understanding of the Christian faith and will be brought "unto the measure of the stature of the fulness of Christ" (Eph. 4:13).

COUNSELING AND THEOLOGY

The pastor-counselor needs to do a thorough study of theology, so that he will be working within a theological framework that is biblically accurate. His theology must be fully undergirded by the Word of God. If he derives his theology from the literature of secular counseling, he will acquire an incomplete, if not invalid, knowledge of it. Even if he limits his reading to the literature of pastoral counseling, he will acquire an inadequate theology because pastoral counseling literature has, unfortunately, been influenced far more by psychology than by biblical theology. A careful reading of the available literature will reveal that much of it has merely sprinkled sacred sayings on a secular enterprise.

One of the areas to which biblical theology addresses itself to the pastor-counselor is in regard to *the nature of man*. This is an area that is most crucial in counseling. As one studies the literature of counseling and psychotherapy, he discovers that there is a wide divergence in the theories of the nature of man. The Rogerians believe that man is sinless; the Freudians affirm that man is good-less; and the behaviorists suggest that man is will-less. A biblical view of man saves the counselor from the optimism of the Rogerians, the pessimism of the Freudians, and the neutralism of the behaviorists.

Another crucial area to which biblical theology addresses itself to the pastor-counselor is regarding *the existence, nature, and activity of God*. If one limits his reading to books on counseling and psychotherapy, he will find that God is often denied, sometimes tolerated, but usually ignored. Of course the pastor-counselor cannot accept any or all of these views, for he knows that the God of the Bible is actively at work in history as well as in human experience. A knowledge of biblical theology relating both to man and to God will enable the

Christian counselor to know *what* man is and that God deals with man *where* he is and *as* he is.

✳ THE WORTH OF PERSONS

There is a basic concept in the teaching of Jesus which has great bearing on pastoral counseling. That concept is the worth of persons. This concept affected much of what Jesus said and did. Jesus affirmed that man was of more value than the entire world. Oxnam says,

> Jesus believed that personality was of supreme value. He put men before things. The question of right and wrong was decided in reference to His estimate of the worth of persons. To enrich personality is to do good. To destroy personality is to do wrong. Man is of infinite worth.[1]

Again he says, "Men, and not things, are the goal of social living."[2] Jesus' teaching reveals the great importance He placed upon the individual. He was not concerned primarily with races, nationalities, selected groups, or isolated families as ends in themselves. His interest lay in the individuals who made up these relationships. Brooks says that, to Jesus, "the final unit is man and that unit of value was never out of the soul of Jesus. To deprive Christianity of the importance of persons would be to deprive it of its very life's blood."[3] This concept of personality so captivated the thinking of Jesus that He made it the end of human action. The golden rule reflects that principle clearly: "As ye would that men should do to you, do ye also to them likewise" (Luke 7:31). Thus, Oxnam points out, "Jesus made man the goal of social living."[4] Jesus viewed things lightly but viewed persons highly. Man was not a thing to be used but a person to be respected. Scott says, "For Jesus men have value in the sight of God not merely as units of society but as personal beings."[5]

Perhaps this parable of Jesus reflects better than any His personal concept of the worth of man:

> And he spake this parable unto them, saying, What man of you, having an hundred sheep, if he lose one of

[handwritten margin notes:] A good idea—could fit in here. (worth in this chapter:: important, not past, present)

them, doth not leave the ninety and nine in the wilderness, and go after that which is lost, until he find it? And when he hath found it, he layeth it on his shoulders, rejoicing. And when he cometh home, he calleth together his friends and neighbours, saying unto them, Rejoice with me; for I have found my sheep which was lost. I say unto you, that likewise joy shall be in heaven over one sinner that repenteth, more than over ninety and nine just persons, which need no repentance (Luke 15:3-7).

To the task of seeking the lost sheep Jesus dedicated himself. The lost sheep was worth seeking for, living for, and dying for.

Jesus was firmly convinced that the individual was more important than the group. As Scott says, "Jesus does not think in terms of masses but in terms of the individual."[6] Bogardus expresses a similar thought by saying, "He dealt with personalities rather than with institutions. He looked to the individual rather than to the mass."[7] Not only was the worth of persons a concept that Christ taught; it was a principle that He commanded His disciples to follow. The ideal of Christ's teaching was that one should become so selfless in his outlook that one's action was of a benevolent nature to individuals irrespective of their social status. The following is expressive of this point,

When saw we thee a stranger, and took thee in? or naked, and clothed thee? Or when saw we thee sick, or in prison, and came unto thee? And the King shall answer and say unto them, Verily I say unto you, Inasmuch as ye have done it unto one of the least of these my brethren, ye have done it unto me (Matt. 25:38-40).

The story of Zacchaeus, the publican, is a good illustration of Jesus' concern for persons. The publicans were a class of people who were abhorred by everyone else. The worst name that could be given to an individual was "publican." Jesus saw value in Zacchaeus no matter what others thought, and determined to go to his home and eat with him. He did this at the expense of jeopardizing His status with the onlookers. He saw one who needed the impact of His own life upon him. The response of Christ to Zacchaeus' joyful reception of Him was, "The Son of man is come to seek and to save that which was lost" (Luke 19:10).

Consider the lepers. They were outcasts from society because of their disease. Not having the advantage of our modern leper colonies, the lepers of Bible times had to separate themselves from the rest of society by crying, "Unclean," so that people near them would not be contaminated. Christ did not reject them because of their condition. He received them and healed them. He recognized their worth.

One of the first disciples of Jesus was Matthew, a tax collector. Because tax collectors worked with the Romans on a commission basis, a fortune could be made by overevaluating property and taxing accordingly. Therefore tax collectors were hated by the people. Jesus, walking by the customs office, saw in Matthew what others did not see—a man—and He made him one of His disciples.

Consider the rich young ruler. This young man possessed many good qualities. He was honest, sincere, and had gained a great deal of prestige. Christ was immediately attracted to him. On the occasion of their meeting, Mark writes, "Jesus beholding him loved him" (Mark 10:21). This love of Christ for the young man was not because of *who* he was but *what* he was—a man.

Love was the key. Jesus' whole life was saturated by love. He demonstrated that love both in His life and in His death. During His life He said, "Love your enemies, bless them that curse you, do good to them that hate you, and pray for them which despitefully use you, and persecute you" (Matt. 5:44). From the Cross, He looked down upon those who had crucified Him and said, "Father, forgive them; for they know not what they do" (Luke 23:34).

What does all of this say to the pastor-counselor? It says that pastors must prize personality as Jesus prized it; that the individual becomes the motivation for, and the sphere of, all pastoral work.

3

Positive and Negative Factors in Pastoral Counseling

THE CULTURAL IMAGE OF THE MINISTER

Ministers do more counseling than any other professional group. This is primarily because of the cultural image of the minister. Persons come to ministers with their problems because they are viewed by many as occupying positions of prestige and respect in the community. Historically ministers have been considered both willing and qualified to help people in crisis. Though there has been a marked change in the general attitude of society toward ministers, the ministry is still considered a profession of dignity and respect. Persons come to a particular pastor because they feel he is an embodiment of a respected profession. They have confidence in both his character as a person and his competence as a counselor— to say nothing of his image as a man of God. The cultural image of a minister creates both opportunity and responsibility for the pastor. Many will come to him for the single reason that he *is* a pastor, and thus many opportunities for helping people are afforded him. However these great opportunities also mean that he has great responsibility, not only to the persons he counsels, but to the profession he represents.

Although counseling is a relatively new professional discipline, it has flourished rapidly and developed many branches. Pastoral counseling is one of the branches that has mushroomed out of the counseling movement. While there are some basic elements that are common to all branches of counseling, there is also disparity among them. In some ways pastoral counseling might be said to be superior to other types of counseling and in other ways it might be said to be inferior. As we compare it with other types, it can be seen that it has both strengths and weaknesses.

Strengths of Pastoral Counseling

1. *Built-in rapport.* The pastoral counselor is one step ahead of other counselors in that, in most cases, he is already acquainted with his counselees. This means that the establishment of rapport, which is so crucial to any kind of counseling, is already attained because of the very nature of the pastor-parishioner relationship. Persons who come to their pastor for counseling do so knowing in advance that they can trust him, that he loves them, and that he is greatly concerned about their well-being. This is not so in most other types of counseling, in which rapport must be achieved *during* the counseling process. Persons seeking other counselors often do so with many misgivings. In fact, these very misgivings often keep them from seeking the help they need; or if they do seek it, they fail to continue with it long enough. Persons often make appointments at counseling centers which they do not keep, or they will go for one interview and not return. While it cannot be said that this always reflects a distrust of counseling, or the counselor, a substantial amount of it does. This is not so in pastoral counseling.

When one goes to a counselor he may not know, he spends considerable time at first testing the counselor to discover if he can be trusted. Persons who come to their pastor for counseling do so with the confidence already established that he will be able to help them and that he can be trusted with their problems. This is a distinct advantage that he has over other types of counselors.

2. *Availability of the pastor.* Parishioners know that ministers are available at any time of the day or night. While this may place a great deal of inconvenience upon the pastor, it affords the parishioner "24-hour service." Although some parishioners take advantage of this availability, this inconvenience is more than offset by knowing that he has the privilege and opportunity of helping his people when they need it most.

3. *Counseling is free.* To say that counseling is free may appear to be somewhat facetious but it is not. The fact that it is free does not simply mean a monetary saving for the parishioner. It means that he receives help that he otherwise would not receive. Many people do not think in terms of paying for counseling services. They would readily part with their money to pay for plumbing, painting, medical or dental services, but do not think in terms of paying for counseling. Thus the problem is not with the *price* of counseling but rather with the *idea* of paying for this kind of service.

4. *The spiritual dimension.* Pastoral counseling is unique in that it gives a great place to the spiritual dimension. It accepts the belief that man is a spiritual being as well as a physical and intellectual one. This broader, biblical view of man keeps the pastor from the "Six Blind Men of Hindustan" fallacy that sees man only in part and not as a whole.

A word of caution should be inserted here. Not only does the general counseling field overlook the spiritual dimension of man; pastoral-counseling literature is too greatly influenced by the literature of secular counseling and thus does not properly emphasize this important aspect. The pastor, while being a diligent student of counseling literature in general and of pastoral counseling in particular, will need to evaluate both of these in the light of the biblical view of man. Failing to do so, he will become merely another secular counselor, abandoning the very area that is his unique domain.

5. *The supernatural aspect.* Recognizing the spiritual dimension of man, both the pastor and the parishioner find it easy to believe that the supernatural is available in the solution of human problems. While God should not be viewed as the easy way out of human dilemmas, He can be viewed as the best way out of them. This means that both the pastor and the parishioner believe that God is at work in human personality and human relationships and that His resources can be utilized as one seeks earnestly to resolve his problem. The Holy Spirit brings illumination and insight to the counseling relationship, making it a truly spiritual experience for both pastor and parishioner. Accepting the spiritual dimension of man, and the belief that the supernatural element can be called upon in the counseling process, makes it natural and appropriate for prayer to be employed. The pastor finds it easy and natural to pray for the parishioner before and following counseling and to pray with him in the midst of the counseling process.

6. *The choice of a Christian counselor.* Persons come to a pastor because he *is* a pastor, because he is a representative for God, because he upholds the precepts of the Bible, and because they believe that the Christian faith which he believes, preaches, and lives has something to say to the problems with which they are dealing. Thus their choice of a Christian counselor is a deliberate one because they feel that he is able to help in a way that other counselors cannot.

Weaknesses of Pastoral Counseling

1. *The parishioner's admission of failure.* Many persons fail to come for pastoral counseling because, by doing so,

they feel that they are admitting failure in living the Christian life. They believe that, had they been the kind of Christians they should, there would not be the necessity for seeking counseling. This is not a limitation of pastoral counseling, as such, however, but it does hinder a pastor from rendering the help that he otherwise could.

2. *The parishioner's embarrassment.* This is closely related to the matter of the parishioner's admission of failure. Many times parishioners are embarrassed to reveal problems in their lives to the one who has perhaps known them as victorious and exemplary Christians. They feel that this will make them appear to be less than Christian and less than what the pastor has viewed them to be in the past. While the pastor does not hold such lofty views of perfection for his parishioners, they sometimes *feel* that he does; and so they find it difficult, if not impossible, to share some secrets of the heart with him.

3. *Fear of exposure.* In many cases persons do not go to their pastors with their problems because of the fear of exposure. This is most unfortunate. While one does not like to think so, many of them have valid reasons for this fear of exposure. Some pastors are known to have leaky tongues. They have been known to be unable to keep a secret, persons who cannot keep a trust. Also, parishioners are aware that many pastors use counseling situations as sermon illustrations. They fear that their problem could become an illustration in a forthcoming sermon. No parishioner wants to be exposed to fellow members in his congregation in this manner. If a parishioner knows that his pastor is the kind who "personalizes" his sermons, even if anonymously, he has no assurance that his problem would not be revealed to the congregation were he to share it with him. Thus the fear of exposure keeps him from receiving the help that he wants and needs.

4. *The pastor's lack of training.* This book has noted the multiple-faceted nature of the pastoral ministry, and the fact

that pastoral counseling is only one of many tasks that the pastor performs. In the course of his training, he receives a certain amount of instruction in counseling, but this does not equip him to be as skilled as a professional counselor whose training for his single task may be as long and intensive as is the pastor's training for all of his tasks. The pastor's lack of training is the greatest weakness of pastoral counseling. Because his training is limited he cannot be expected to know the work as well as one who has spent many years studying and practicing it. Also, in most cases a pastor does not have the benefit of clinical training which exposes him to human problems at their deepest level. The professional counselor receives this kind of training and he has the benefit not only of seeing these deep problems but of working with them under the skilled guidance of a qualified teacher. Much of a pastor's knowledge of counseling is acquired through the trial-and-error method. While the value of experience cannot be denied, neither can it be said that experience alone qualifies the pastor to be the kind of counselor that he needs to be in this complex society.

His training does not give him a knowledge of how to give, score, and interpret tests. While it cannot be said that tests can reveal totally valid data about human personality, they do afford a great insight into it. Without the benefit of knowledge that can come from the use of tests, the pastor becomes seriously hampered as he attempts to deal with some problems.

It has been stated that pastoral counseling has both strengths and weaknesses, but the strengths outweigh the weaknesses. Therefore the pastor should make the most of his strengths while, at the same time, trying to improve in the areas of weakness. While realizing that his limitations should afford him an appropriate sense of modesty, he should, at the same time, be fully aware that he can deal with some problems better than other counselors.

Counseling Across the Gap

Sometimes a pastor becomes aware of a disturbing gap in the counseling process. The gap is not between himself and his parishioner; rather, it is between the pastor's real self and his ideal self. Of course this gap is present in all pastors and all parishioners and it is one with which every sensitive Christian deals. What makes it especially threatening and guilt-producing to the pastor is that the parishioner is trying to close the gap in his own life in the presence of a minister who knows deep within himself that he is struggling with much the same kind of problem.

The pastor is likely to feel somewhat hypocritical because he knows many parishioners believe he has reached the ideal. While he knows that this is not so, nor has he claimed it to be so, he nevertheless feels somewhat phony as he engages in the counseling process. (This is also felt when he is preaching, but that cannot be dealt with here.) This places him in the awkward and embarrassing position of "counseling across the gap." Let it be understood that the reference here is not to sin, which is defined as a willful transgression of the known law of God. Rather, it has to do with the process of growing in the Christian life and struggling with the deeper implications of Christian faith.

Two broad options are open to the pastor who becomes aware of this gap: (1) deny that the gap exists or (2) admit it to himself and to God. The former is debilitating; the latter is liberating. The former forces the pastor to protect a kind of self that does not really exist; the latter releases him to be the struggling saint that he really is. The former causes him to assume a false position of superiority over his counselee, tempting him to manipulate or look down on him; the latter lets him be on a level with his parishioner, releasing him to relate to him and reach across to him.

4

Counseling, a Function
of the Ministry

THE NATURE OF THE PASTORAL MINISTRY

The minister is called to serve an age that is gripped not
only by the problems that have always confronted men but
also with a plethora of problems that plague this present gen-
eration. Among the latter are such things as: (1) the threat of
starvation for millions due to the population explosion; (2) the
danger of annihilation through nuclear warfare; (3) the threats
of revolts by youth having their adolescence complicated by
society's uncertainty whether to be permissive or authoritarian, and so it is both; (4) the problem of affluence resulting
in a materialism that causes men to be practical polytheists by
making idols of things; (5) the tragedy of the rapid dissolu-
tion of the home; (6) the problem of the education explosion
that has caused some to be educated beyond their wisdom;

and (7) the problem of a secularity which ignores God and makes the Church seem irrelevant and unnecessary.

It is to this kind of world that the pastor is called. To this kind of age he must minister meaningfully. The pastoral ministry can best be understood as resting upon a trinity of premises: (1) it is *of* God; (2) it is *by* the Holy Spirit; and (3) it is *for* people.

1. *It Is of God*

That the ministry is of God cannot be debated by any serious student of the Word. Throughout both the Old and New Testaments this is affirmed. A pastor must never escape the profound truth that he is called of God to do God's work in God's way. A clear, biblical view of his call and of the Church's mission will, as Jowett says, "save us from becoming small officials in transient enterprises. It will make us truly big, and will, therefore, save us from spending our days in trifling."[1] It will also enable him to give himself to activity that is aimed toward the fulfillment of Christ's mission for the Church. How much pastoral "administrivia" would be eliminated if pastors would keep a clear view that their work is of God and that their work must always be guided by the objectives He has advanced for His Church!

The Bible is not silent about the character of the minister nor about the nature of the ministry. The following references are given to show this biblical perspective:

A man must be of blameless reputation, he must be married to one wife only, and be a man of self-control and discretion. He must be a man of disciplined life; he must be hospitable and have the gift of teaching. He must neither be intemperate nor violent, but gentle. He must not be a controversialist nor must he be fond of money-grabbing. He must have proper authority in his own household, and be able to control and command the respect of his children. (For is a man cannot rule his own house how can he look after the Church of God?) He must not be a beginner in the faith, for fear of his becoming conceited

39

and sharing the devil's downfall. He should, in addition to the above qualifications, have a good reputation with the outside world (I Tim. 3:2-7, Phillips).

And from St. Peter:

> I urge you then to see that your "flock of God" is properly fed and cared for. Accept the responsibility of looking after them willingly and not because you feel you can't get out of it, doing your work not for what you can make, but because you are really concerned for their well-being. You should aim not at being "little tin gods" but as examples of Christian living in the eyes of the flock committed to your charge. And then, when the chief shepherd reveals himself, you will receive that crown of glory which cannot fade (I Pet. 5:2-4, Phillips).

A small girl was drawing a picture with her crayons. Her mother asked her whose picture she was drawing. "God's," she answered. Her mother replied, "But, Dear, nobody knows what He looks like." The little girl responded, "They will when I'm finished." When a pastor has concluded his ministry in a given church, people should know what God looks like because they have seen His picture in the pastor's work. If his ministry is *of* God, it will *portray* God.

A man who is firmly convinced that his ministry is of God will be saved from the struggle for status that captures the attention of many contemporary pastors. Much has been written recently of the "identity crisis" faced by ministers. It is granted that, societally, the minister suffers from lack of an adequate definition of his role. No alert pastor can escape the implications of the multiplicity of role expectations imposed upon him by a society uncertain of what his work should be.

Recently the Educational Testing Service sent a questionnaire to 1,000 lay leaders in various denominations asking them to give their concept of "an outstanding minister." The data was turned over to a group of psychological testers and they were asked to determine who was being described. Their answer was, "A junior vice-president of Sears Roebuck."[2]

William E. Hulme said, "The minister suffers from a sense of professional inferiority. In his own mind he is low man on the professional totem pole."[3] This being so, many ministers yearn to be recognized as equals to the doctor, the lawyer, the psychiatrist, and the psychologist. In this they reflect the culture's enormous preoccupation with labels. Let it be asserted that if the ministry ever gains equal status with the other professions, it will be a step-down for the ministry.

Perhaps ministers should be made aware of the findings of a comprehensive study made a few years ago by the Joint Commission on Mental Health. In response to the question, "Where do you go for help with a personal problem?" the responses were as follows: 42 percent went to clergymen, 29 percent to doctors, 18 percent to psychiatrists or psychologists, 13 percent to social-service agencies, 6 percent to lawyers, 3 percent to marriage counselors, and 1 percent to others such as teachers, nurses, policemen, and judges.[4]

It was further determined by the study that the outcomes were as favorable, if not more so, for persons consulting a clergyman as for those who had sought the services of other professionals. The minister should realize that in the minds of many he *already* possesses the status which he so earnestly desires. Perhaps he should give his attention to matters that really matter. If a minister is desirous for a label, what is wrong with the label "servant of God"? For what else could one wish?

2. *It Is by the Holy Spirit*

This is not to be construed to mean that it is the Spirit's ministry *apart* from the minister; rather it is *through* the minister. The Early Church placed a high premium upon the Spirit-filled ministry, even for persons chosen to minister in subordinate positions. In the Acts of the Apostles the instruction was given that the deacons should be men "full of the Holy Ghost" (Acts 6:3). The Holy Spirit literally called Barnabas and Saul by saying, "Separate me Barnabas and Saul for the work whereunto I have called them" (Acts 13:3). The record is that they were "sent forth by the Holy Ghost" (Acts 13:4).

Sanders says, "Spiritual leadership can be exercised only by Spirit-filled men. Other qualifications are desirable. This is indispensable."[5] He also says, "Spirituality is not easy to define but its presence or absence can be easily discerned."[6]

A Spirit-less ministry is like a handless glove; it has shape but not substance. The pastor who attempts to minister meaningfully to persons wrestling with the raw realities of contemporary society very quickly bankrupts his own human resources. He is confronted with the knowledge that he must draw heavily upon the resources of the Holy Spirit if he is to minister with any degree of adequacy.

A pastor can look into the face of his gathered church on any Lord's Day and see reflected there problems whose number is exceeded only by their depth. In a congregation of any size, persons can be found who are guilt-ridden; persons whose lives are meaningless; the youthful who are caught in the storms and stresses of adolescence; the aged who are facing the imminency of their own passing; the frightened, the lonely, and the unloved. To all of these—the disinherited, the disenchanted, the disheartened, and the dismayed—the pastor must minister. How great a task he has, and how greatly does he need the power of the Holy Spirit in his life!

A few years ago this writer was confronted with a question from which he cannot escape. It is given here in the hope that it will disturb others as it has disturbed him. Dr. Carl Bates asked, "What are you doing that you can't get done unless the power of God falls on your ministry?"[7]

3. It Is for People

A minister once said to his psychotherapist, "My life is characterized by a plethora of contacts and a poverty of relationships."[8] How true this is for many ministers! The contacts will automatically exist by the very nature of the ministry, but the relationships arising out of those contacts are solely the creation of the minister. The depth of a man's ministry is measured by the depth of his interpersonal relationships with his people. Out of relationships arise both agony and ecstasy for the pastor, but there is more ecstasy than agony.

One of the most tragic mistakes a pastor can make is failing to recognize the worth of persons. It is the darkest day in a pastor's life when he looks at a person and sees a "thing." Things can be used, but people are to be loved. How subtle is the temptation for a pastor to dominate his people rather than serve them! Seneca said, "Wherever there is a human being there is an opportunity for a kindness." A Japanese proverb says, "One kind word can warm three winter months." The success of a pastor is determined, not by the number of people he has, but by the number of people he serves.

Many ministers have an "edifice-complex" which makes them place church buildings high on their list of loves. How concerned many pastors are that their buildings be large enough to hold their crowds! Of greater concern should be the question, Do I have room for these people in my heart?

If one would serve people, he must begin by understanding them. Lindgren said, "The deeper his understanding of persons and the closer his pastoral relationship to them, the more effective he will be in speaking to them meaningfully."[9] As Clinebell put it, "The only relevance that really matters is relevance to the deep needs of persons."[10] One woman said to her counselor, "Every person is someone calling for help." To these cries a pastor must respond. To fail to respond to persons is to deny their personhood.

Jesus set the pattern in the parable of the Good Samaritan. Is it not strange that of the three persons who saw the wounded man—the priest, the Levite, and the Samaritan— it was the last, a non-clergyman, who was the only one who ministered? It is sad that the priest and the Levite were too busy carrying out their ministry (whatever it was) to minister. It has been said, "We pretend to love everybody, and by a generalized loving of everybody, we avoid the deep grasp of an I-thou relationship. We substitute the glad hand of making friends and influencing people for the intensity of a caring relationship."[11]

In his Gospel, Mark asserts that the one who holds the prominent position must be everybody's slave, and he buttressed that argument with the reminder that our Lord "came not to be ministered unto, but to minister" (Mark 10:45).

In conclusion, let it be reaffirmed that the pastoral ministry rests upon this trinity of premises: (1) it is *of* God; (2) it is *by* the Holy Spirit; and (3) it is *for* people. Leave out the "of God" aspect and the ministry becomes a choice, not a call. Leave out the "by the Spirit" aspect and the ministry becomes an exercise of humanity, not an enterprise with Deity. Leave out the "for people" aspect and the ministry becomes a manipulation, not a mediation.

THE PLACE OF COUNSELING IN THE PASTORAL MINISTRY

Because of the nature of the pastoral ministry, a minister must be a generalist, not a specialist. When a pastor begins to "specialize" in any facet of the ministry, it is likely that other aspects of his work will suffer. Many things are required of a contemporary pastor: praying, studying, preaching, teaching, planning, organizing, administering, calling, counseling, plus a myriad of other duties. The pastoral tasks are so many and so diverse as to make it both undesirable and unwise for a minister to single out any one of them and give undue attention to it.

A pastor must learn to budget his time so that one activity does not absorb an inordinate amount of his time. Pastors who elect to specialize in any single function of the ministry do not have a proper perception of the pastoral ministry. The nearest thing to a specialty in pastoral work should be preaching, but even this worthy objective is not without its pitfalls. Pastors can so center their time and attention in preparation for preaching that they cloister themselves away from their people. A shepherd who is not in constant contact with his sheep is not a shepherd.

Counseling is an important part of the ministry but it is not all-important. A pastor who devotes too much time to counseling not only has a lack of understanding of the pastoral ministry; he is likely also to have an improper evaluation of his counseling skills. Some who view themselves as good counselors may not deserve that self-rating at all, causing them to over-engage in counseling as a compensation for inadequacies in other pastoral tasks. They "advertise" their counseling ministry, which results in an increased counseling load. This "justifies" a lack of time and attention given to other pastoral tasks.

Most pastors will be involved in as much counseling as they want, or need, without labeling themselves as "specialists" in that area. A great disadvantage of spending too much time in counseling is that the few absorb so much of the pastor's time and energy that he is not able to minister adequately to the many. If a few people continuously demand an inordinate amount of the pastor's time, it is likely that the church as a whole will be hurt while only a few are being helped. It is better to be known as a pastor who counsels rather than a counselor who pastors. Someone has counted the times the New Testament records that Jesus counseled and found the number to be 35. Yet Jesus was known as a Preacher-Teacher. The contemporary pastor cannot improve on that.

While it is possible for a pastor to spend too much time in counseling, it is also true that he can spend too little time in that activity. Some pastors have a distaste for counseling, causing them to avoid as many counseling situations as possible. Some have an outright disdain for it, assuming that if their parishioners had a proper religious experience counseling would not be necessary. Some have a distrust of their skill in this area and thus are fearful of entering counseling relationships with their people. Some have a fear of the raw realities of life that may be unearthed and so are hesitant to enter into in-depth counseling experiences.

The bench and the chair. Some pastors, particularly those in the evangelical tradition, cannot see the relationship between the mourners' bench and the counseling chair. They believe that the need for counseling seems to negate what can, and does, happen at an altar of prayer. Broadly conceived, many assume that the mourners' bench is a symbol of conservative theology while the counseling chair is a symbol of liberal theology. However, this is an unnecessary and unrealistic labeling which results in unfortunate polarity. In reality, the mourners' bench and the counseling chair are not competitive; they are complementary. Many persons whose repentance is genuine, whose consecration is clear, and whose Christian service and witness are unquestioned, still need to work through some theological questions and problems of Christian living in a counseling situation. Both the pastor who is aware of this and the layman who is not threatened by it are released to give their energies to the pursuit of the answers to these problems without feeling that it is a denial of the faith of the layman, an admission of ineffectiveness of the minister, or an insult to the theological tradition of both.

Disadvantages of too much counseling:

1. It limits to the few the pastor's ministry which is needed by the many.

2. It affords neurotic parishioners too much opportunity to gain the attention they want rather than making the changes they need.

3. It keeps the pastor from engaging in other pastoral tasks which are equally, if not more, important.

Disadvantages of too little counseling:

1. It prevents parishioners from receiving the help they need through pastoral counseling.

2. It isolates the pastor from the raw realities of life which his people are experiencing.

3. It prevents the development of warm interpersonal relationships between pastor and people which can emerge from counseling relationships.

Guidelines for the pastor:

A pastor can keep his counseling ministry in proper perspective in the following ways:

1. Keeping aware of *all* of his responsibilities, so that he does not allow too much time to be absorbed in counseling activities.

2. Keeping each counseling interview to a maximum length of an hour, except in rare cases.

3. Spacing interviews with any one person a week apart, so that the parishioner has time to apply to his problem the insights and learnings from previous interviews.

4. Recognizing that many neurotics are seeking to gain attention, not to find solutions to their problems.

5. Referring parishioners to other persons or agencies when their problems lie beyond his competency.

COUNSELING AND PREACHING

Broadly conceived, preaching can do three things as related to counseling: (1) it can close the door to counseling; (2) it can open the door to counseling; and (3) it can obviate the need for counseling.

Whether his preaching closes or opens the door to counseling depends on two factors: (1) the pastor's attitude and (2) the preaching content. The attitude of the pastor which is projected through his preaching determines to a great extent the amount of counseling he will do. If in his preaching his attitude is hard, cold, and judgmental, his hearers will immediately sense that he is not the kind of person with whom they can speak about the intimate aspects of their lives. (Of course, the attitude of the pastor is revealed in relationships other than preaching, but it shows through more clearly there than anywhere else.) If, on the other hand, his preaching is characterized by warmth, tenderness, and understanding, his people will feel that he can be approached with any kind of problem, knowing that he will accept them. Unfortunately, some pastors equate gentleness with weakness and they feel that such an attitude is a denial of the demands of the gospel. However, an examination of the preaching of Jesus will dispel such a belief, for the New Testament clearly shows that He presented the most piercing truth with great love.

The preaching content also tends to determine the amount of counseling a pastor will do. If preaching is judgmental (full of law), it drives parishioners from the pastor; if it is compassionate (full of grace), it draws them to him. Jackson says:

> When the words from the pulpit are obviously the effort of a person-conscious pastor to mediate the healing love of God, he will open the doors of people's hearts, as well as open the doors to his counseling room. For effective preaching will always be an invitation to go further in the exploring of personal needs. [12]

Preaching can obviate the need for many counseling situations by properly ministering to the needs of persons out of the deep resources of God's love and grace. Preaching at its best shows how the great gap between the weakness of humanity and the standards of Deity can be spanned by the bridge of grace. Thus, preaching is both confrontational and mediational, two elements which are also present in a sound counseling relationship.

This does not mean that preaching can obviate the need for *all* counseling, but it does mean that the kinds of problems that can be solved by preaching should be resolved in that manner.

5

Techniques of Counseling

The pastor-counselor need not commit himself to a certain theory, school, or approach to counseling. No one theory has proved to be effective in all situations or even in specific types of situations. Therefore there is no single "right" way to counsel. Actually, many approaches or theories may be right; that is, they may prove to be effective in certain situations, while at other times apparently no theory or approach seems to be satisfactory.

As one studies the literature of counseling, it becomes readily apparent that there is a wide range of theories from which to choose. The earnest counselor will seek to learn as many approaches as possible, in the knowledge that at certain times he will need to employ an approach which he does not customarily use. The nearest thing to the "right" approach to use is the one which the counselor has found to be most effective and the one with which he is most comfortable. Just as a highly proficient pianist utilizes the whole keyboard as he plays, so the pastor should be acquainted with the full keyboard of counseling techniques, so that he can employ the portion he wishes to use as the need arises.

Counseling is concerned with the process of change in the counselee. It is most interesting to note that all of the schools of counseling have the common objective of creating change in the counselees, but their methodologies are markedly different in reaching that objective.

NONDIRECTIVE AND DIRECTIVE COUNSELING

Broadly conceived, all methods of counseling range between two extremes, namely, nondirective and directive counseling. The nondirective approach is a counselee-centered approach, whereas the directive approach is a counselor-centered approach. In the nondirective approach the person becomes the focus of the counseling process, whereas in the directive approach the problem is the focus. In the nondirective method the emphasis is upon learning, namely, the learning that is achieved by the counselee, whereas in the directive method the emphasis is upon teaching, the teaching that is done by the counselor.

In the nondirective view the basis for change is that of insight achieved by the counselee; however, in the directive view the basis for change is reason.. The nondirective theory centers its emphasis upon the dimension of the affective, which is that of feeling and emotion. In the directive theory the emphasis is upon the cognitive, which has to do with perceiving and knowing. In the nondirective approach the process is done *with* the individual, whereas in the directive approach the process of counseling is *for* the individual.

The attitude of the nondirective style is that of democracy, whereas the directive style is the attitude of authority.

The nondirective counselor engages in little interpretation, whereas the directive counselor does a great deal of interpreting. The nondirective counselor assumes little responsibility for the topic of conversation, whereas the directive counselor assumes much responsibility for it.

The nondirective approach to counseling may be more appropriately called client-centered theory. It began in 1942 when Carl Rogers published a book entitled *Counseling and Psychotherapy*. This book was Rogers' attempt to theorize his own psychotherapeutic approach. As a practicing psychotherapist he came to see that the interview is the breeding ground for the insights that the counselee receives. Therefore the important aspect of counseling is the subjective nature of the client-counselor interaction. Rogers has never stated his theory as fact, although some of his followers have done so. His theory has changed and is changing. When he first presented his nondirective approach, he presented it in an extreme form. However, since that time, he has changed the theory to give occasion for more counselor activity in the counseling process.

One of the distinctive characteristics of the Rogerian or nondirective approach is the conception of man. Rogers believes in the democratic ideal, namely, the dignity and worth of the individual. He feels that man has a right to his opinion, to his own destiny, to freedom and independence, and to self-direction. He feels that man is predominately a subjective creature who lives in an objective world. He believes that in every person there is a tendency toward actualization. By this he means that inherently man moves toward growth, health, adjustment, socialization, self-realization, independence, and autonomy. He believes that man is trustworthy and therefore basically good. "Evil" arises out of defenses which alienate man from his inherent nature. Rogers also believes that man is wiser than his intellect. By this he means that when man is functioning non-defensively, the intuitive combines with the cognitive, making the total greater than conscious thinking alone.

Rogers believes that man exists in a changing world of experience of which he is the center. Man's private world is called the phenomenal field or experiential field and can be known only by the individual himself. Man reacts to this field as it is experienced and perceived, and this perceptual field is reality. Behavior, in Rogers' view, is the attempt of man to satisfy his needs as experienced and perceived. Man reacts, not to reality, but to his perceptions of reality. Reality to him is, in effect, perceptions of reality whether or not they have been confirmed.

It is believed by Rogers that behavior is best understood from the individual's "internal frame of reference." This term means all of one's experiences, sensations, perceptions, emotions, and meanings at any given moment of consciousness. Counseling seeks to know this internal frame of reference by concentrating on the counselee's subjective reality. Rogers feels that in this process empathy is needed. When empathy is felt by the counselor, the counselee is viewed as a person. However, if the counselee is viewed from the external frame of reference, the tendency is to treat him as an object.

Rogers believes that most behavior is consistent with one's self-concept. The self-concept is one's view of himself in relation to other persons and things. The self-concept is fluid and changing but at any given moment it is a fixed entity. He feels that maladjustment results from defensive maneuvers to keep perceptions of behavior consistent with the self-concept.

Rogers talks about what he calls incongruence or dissociation. He believes that this results when there is a rift between the self-concept and the self-experiences. This originates in the early years, when the child needs much love from his parents and others. This love from parents or others is made conditional; that is, the child receives love if he behaves as they require. Thus, he lives by values that are not his own.

They are contrary to his normal process of evaluating his experience. Therefore the child tries to actualize a self that is contradictory or incongruent with the organismic processes of his actualizing tendency. Rogers feels that when one is living by values introjected from others he is living under the conditions of worth. That is, he becomes worthy (worth something) when he is doing that which others want him to do. This means that he is living his life by the values of others rather than by the values that are his own.

Client-centered theory holds that when experience contradicts self-concept, and one is aware of it, a state of anxiety exists. In other words, perceived incongruence threatens the self-concept and anxiety results. Thus one denies the experience or mis-perceives it to make it more consistent with the self-concept. This protects him but distorts reality. Change comes about by creating conditions where there is less threat and less need to resist. Rogers believes that a corrective relationship (counseling) with another person can decrease the necessity to act upon the conditions of worth and increase one's positive self-regard. The aim therefore is to relax, little by little, the boundaries of the client's self-concept, so that it may assimilate denied and distorted experiences. In this way the self becomes more congruent with experience.

Rogers believes that every person should be a fully functioning person. The fully functioning person may be viewed as the ideally adjusted person who is open to all of his experiences; that is, he exhibits no defensiveness, he does not live under conditions of worth, and he experiences unconditional positive regard. His self-concept is congruent with his experience and he acts in terms of his basic actualizing tendency which actualizes the self. As he meets life situations his self-structure assimilates them.

It is apparent that Rogerian theory does not have the support of the Bible. Man is not, in fact, basically good. Man is not trustworthy. This means, then, that the pastor cannot appropriate all of the Rogerian theory. However there are many valid and valuable insights that the Rogerian approach offers the pastor. While it cannot be said that Rogers' theory of man is biblical, it can be said that his theory of the *value* of human personality is biblical. The Rogerian approach prizes human personality. It places much emphasis upon the worth of persons. For that reason, this aspect of the Rogerian approach will be often utilized in pastoral counseling.

In sharp contrast to the nondirective approach is the directive approach, which is the older form of counseling. This is the approach to counseling that has been used for centuries. In this approach the counselor becomes the central figure, who poses as an authority, one who knows the answers to persons' problems. In this approach the counselor functions primarily as an advisor or an information-giver; he assumes a teaching role. The directive approach assumes that the counselor has greater knowledge, greater experience, and greater insight than the counselee. This means that the counselor tends to counsel "down" to the counselee rather than "across to" (with) the counselee. He tends to act as a diagnostician who presumes to know both the disease and the cure. There is a sense in which the directive counselor operates from a position of conceit. He appears to have the answers to all questions. Therefore he needs only an understanding of the problem in order to prescribe a cure for it.

It can readily be seen that in this process the counselee is not greatly involved. His major role as counselee is to verbalize his problem. Once the problem is known to the counselor, he proceeds to furnish the advice which is needed to solve the problem. Many pastors will find it easy, almost natural, to engage in this form of counseling. This is because the position of the minister is viewed by many as being an authority figure. Pastors who are insecure will find great refuge in that position of authority. They will find it much easier to talk down to their parishioners than to work with them. When a pastor is talking down to people he is not really becoming involved with them. This means that he is not truly experiencing what they are experiencing and he does not fully understand what they are feeling. This is the reason why many persons refuse to go to a pastor for counseling. They do not want to be "preached at" at short range.

Most of the time the pastor will be operating somewhere between the two extremes of nondirective and directive counseling. By not committing himself to either extreme he can utilize the values of both approaches while at the same time avoiding their limitations. There will be times when the pastor will be very nondirective. This will be particularly true in the initial stages of the first counseling session with an individual, for it is during this time that the pastor learns what the parishioner is experiencing. He hears him verbalize his problems and attempts to get inside his internal frame of reference, so he can fully understand what is troubling him. While a pastor may begin with the nondirective approach in a counseling interview, it is neither likely nor desirable that he will remain at that end of the continuum. There will be times when he will find it helpful to become quite directive, sharing his feelings and teaching him what he feels he ought to know. Having done so, he will likely move to a middle position, a cooperative approach, in which he works with the counselee in resolving the specific problem. Thus, it is not an either/or choice between the nondirective and directive methods. This unfortunate polarity existed for some time in the counseling field, forcing counselors to choose a method, use it, and defend it. There is no longer the need to continue a battle which should never have been fought in the first place.

OTHER APPROACHES TO COUNSELING

There are two broad categories of therapies: the emotionally oriented (affective) and the intellectually oriented (cognitive). Until recently, the emotionally oriented therapies constituted the bulk of psychotherapeutic systems. However, newer forms of intellectually oriented therapy are emerging, so that the imbalance is not as great. In this section some of the newer approaches to counseling will be briefly examined. The purpose of this discussion is to introduce the pastor to some methods of counseling, parts of which he may employ in his counseling ministry. He will need to make a more thorough study of these systems than this brief introduction will allow before he can adequately employ these methods in his counseling ministry.

1. *Logotherapy*. The originator and chief proponent of this theory is Viktor Frankl. His theory can be found in his four books: *Man's Search for Meaning, Psychotherapy and Existentialism, The Doctor and the Soul,* and *The Will to Meaning*. This theory centers in the concept of the will to meaning. Frankl was imprisoned by the Nazis in World War II, during which time he experienced great suffering and observed others undergoing the same suffering. He believed that many of his fellow prisoners died because they lacked a meaning in life, even under those adverse conditions.

Logotherapy is rooted in anthropology. Man is free to take whatever attitude he chooses toward his existential situation. He can choose to invest meaning and value in whatever confronts him. This "will to meaning" becomes the motivational force in human existence.

Logotherapy gives a large place to the spiritual dimension of man. It is a personalistic psychotherapy which attempts to bring about a change of attitude in a person toward his symptom rather than treating the symptom directly. Thus its emphasis is upon the whole man.

While Frankl does not write from a Christian perspective, the pastor will find that logotherapy parallels Christian thought to a considerable degree. Donald F. Tweedie, who studied under Frankl, has attempted to place logotherapy within the framework of Christian theology. The pastor will find his two books, *Logotherapy and the Christian Faith* and *The Christian and the Couch*, helpful and interesting reading.

2. *Integrity therapy*. This theory was originated by O. Hobart Mowrer, whose theory can be found in two books: *The Crisis in Psychiatry and Religion* and *The New Group Therapy*. It centers in two major areas: guilt and integrity. Disillusioned by the Freudian approach toward resolving guilt, Mowrer, through personal experience, came to see that guilt must be resolved through confession. Integrity therapy is concerned with developing individuals into responsible persons by means of openness (dialogue), confession, and positive action. It holds that each individual is a responsible person with a value system. When that value system (conscience) is violated, guilt arises. The resolution of guilt is not through repression but through confession. Confession leads to restitution.

Integrity therapy uses much Christian terminology such as guilt, sin, confession, and restitution but it is not really a Christian therapy. However, John W. Drakeford has systematized the theory and placed it in the Christian framework. His book entitled *Integrity Therapy* is commended to pastors as a helpful guide in counseling from this theoretical viewpoint.

3. *Transactional analysis*. This theory was advanced by Eric Berne, who wrote *Transactional Analysis in Psychotherapy*. The theory has been further elaborated by Paul McCormick and Leonard Campos in their small book called *Introduce Yourself to Transactional Analysis*, and by Thomas Harris in his book with the interesting title *I'm O.K., You're O.K.*

The theory holds that there are three ego states in each individual: (1) a parent, which feels, talks, and behaves as one's own parents did; (2) an adult, which sorts facts out of feelings; and (3) a child, which feels, talks, and behaves as one did as a child. At any given moment one of these ego states may be in control. The relationships between persons are called transactions (exchanges) between persons. The transactions may be exchanges such as adult to adult, adult to parent, parent to parent, and parent to child. Simple transactions result when the lines of exchange are not crossed; that is, when the ego state in one person is relating and responding to the identical ego state in another person. Crossed transactions, when the ego state in one person is relating and responding to a different ego state in another person, result in a breakdown of communication.

The pastor will find this theory helpful as he engages in marriage and family counseling, particularly the former. The best use of it can be made in group marriage counseling.

4. *Reality therapy*. This approach was originated by William Glasser. In 1965 he published a book entitled *Reality Therapy*, which contains his theory. It is a protest against Freudian psychology's concern with the past. Reality therapy is concerned with the reality of the present and its emphasis is upon responsible behavior. It is more concerned with behavior than with attitudes. The goal of reality therapy is to enable persons to engage in behavior which is characterized by a willingness to accept responsibility for its actions. Reality therapy seeks to aid persons to face life as it really is and to help them face up to the consequences of their own behavior.

The pastor will find that there is much in reality therapy that he can use in his counseling work. It would seem to work best for persons who are strongly motivated to change and who have sufficient ego strength to do so.

5. *Rational therapy*. This therapy was founded by Albert Ellis but its roots reach back into the period of Greek philosophy hundreds of years before Christ. It seeks to enable persons to resolve their problems through reason. Ellis collaborated with Robert Harper and published a book in 1961 entitled *A Guide to Rational Living*. This book outlines the basic assumptions of rational therapy. The basic presupposition of rational therapy is that man's problems are the result of irrational thinking and that his problems can be avoided and resolved by making his behavior conform to reason. It holds that man can live a fulfilling, creative, and emotionally

satisfying life by intelligently organizing and disciplining his thinking.

While there is much in this approach to commend itself to the pastor-counselor, the theory also has much with which he cannot agree. There are at least two reasons for this: (1) it is a humanistic approach which gives no place for the divine dimension; and (2) it denies the power of the emotions to distort reason.

The Process of Pastoral Counseling

A thorough knowledge of counseling techniques is necessary if the minister is to be of real service to his parishioners. If he is unsure about what the process of pastoral counseling is, it will militate against the possibility of his success. Thus, he should be well-versed in the techniques of counseling and he must be able to be "at home" in the counseling process.

There are three factors which affect the approach of the minister toward counseling: (1) his attitudes toward persons and their problems, (2) his religious interpretation of man, and (3) his conception of himself and of his role as a minister. These factors determine the course and quality of the counseling process.

If the minister assumes that he is of greater worth, is more intelligent and of greater moral strength than his parishioners, he may assume an authoritarian attitude in counseling. There may be the temptation to resort to advice-giving rather than to real counseling. He is apt to manipulate the interview by asking direct questions, making interpretations, and offering stock solutions and answers. Carroll Wise warns, "The temptation to display his deeper knowledge verbally must be faced and worked through within himself. The major reason for such display is in the ego satisfaction it gives the counselor."[1] The pastor should not be aggressive, for there is definite harm that can be done by pushing and probing, by confronting the counselee with more than he can handle.

Forcing interpretations on a counselee may create shock and hostility.

"Counseling at its best is . . . a form of creative interaction. It is more than the exchange of opinions,"[2] says Karl Stolz. Thus it must be a cooperative enterprise, one in which there is more than talking; it must be the conveyance of experiences in terms of their meaning. "It is not what the counselor does to or for the counselee that is important; the important thing is what happens between them."[3] This is the very heart of real counseling. May called this the key to the counseling process.[4]

Communication is more than verbalization. Facial expressions, bodily posture, gestures, and other types of conduct are also means of communication. The minister must be aware of what the silent signs tell him.

The task of the counselor is not to interpret; rather, it is to help the counselee make his own interpretations. This means that the counselor must be adept at insight and he must be willing to let the counselee develop this insight, too. Wise called insight "the goal of counseling."[5] A person with a feeling of guilt must be permitted to find full release from it by communicating with the minister, who has created an atmosphere of acceptance and understanding. The pastor-counselor must guard against trying to give verbal reassurances to his counselee. Some psychologists insist that these expressions of reassurance are really expressions of the counselor's own anxieties. Reassurance "is not given by the counselor, but it is rather the result of the two working together in an attempt to find a deeper sense of positive reality in the experiences of the counselee."[6] Reassurance comes as a by-product of the sharing of experience by the pastor and his parishioner.

The pastor must refrain from thrusting his convictions upon his counselee. This is not advisable because it makes the counselor rather than the counselee the focal point of the counseling situation. Hiltner says, "It is plainly wrong if done exploitatively or coercively, because such action would ignore the inherent dignity of the person."[7] Bonnell states it this way: "Whatever confidences are given to him he receives in the spirit of sympathetic understanding. It is not his task to judge people."[8] He should develop a manner of composure to such extent that he will never be shocked by what is told him in confidence. Bonnell has advanced some general principles for the pastor-counselor which are worth consideration. They are:

1. Very few people, whether parishioners or strangers, who come in to talk to the minister, state frankly and clearly at the outset the real purpose of the visit.

2. Listen patiently to the parishioner who has come to talk with you.

3. Do not accept a parishioner's diagnosis of his own problem.

4. Familiarize yourselves with your parishioners' problems so as to develop insight into their basic needs.

5. Every confidence entrusted to us in personal interviews must be kept inviolate.[9]

The attitude of the minister toward his people should be one of respect. As his people learn to trust him, so should he learn to trust his people. His constant attitude toward them should be one that reveals that he has faith in humanity and the latent good that is resident there.

FUNCTIONS OF COUNSELING

1. *Listening*. The counselor should let the birth of the counselee's story occur naturally without domination or coercion. When the pastor attempts to deliver the problem by Caesarean section, there is the possibility of harming the patient. Natural birth of the story is slower, but it involves less risk. The counselee experiences a form of healing as he tells his story at his own rate of speed. It is not easy for many persons to move from isolation to intimacy. When the coun-

selor tries to speed this process he adds to his counselee's anxiety rather than reducing it.

When a pastor is listening well he is being carried on the stream of the counselee's emotion. Like a man floating in a shallow stream, he can let the current carry him but he is always able to "touch bottom." Thus he can get the feeling of the counselee's emotion without being inundated by it. He can be carried by it without being overwhelmed by it.

Many people are not good listeners. Only a small percent of what is said is heard. Yet millions are dying (emotionally) because they are not being heard. One such woman, frustrated because her husband would not listen to her, made this sweeping statement: "Nobody listens to anybody anymore." She was almost right. Our major means of interpersonal contact is through talking. When persons' talk is heard, a form of therapy occurs; when it is not heard, frustration occurs.

The pastor is in a position to aid persons simply by listening to them. Unfortunately, many pastors are not good listeners. This is understandable when we realize that the major thrust of a pastor's training is to help him communicate, not to listen. His extensive study in the biblical, theological, and historical areas, as well as his training in many of the practical areas, equips him to communicate his knowledge to others. Certainly this is of vital importance. Yet while a pastor's effectiveness in the pulpit is dependent upon his ability to talk (to communicate truth), much of his effectiveness in the parish is dependent upon his ability to listen.

Many pastors cannot easily make the transition from talking to hearing. Failing in this, they cripple their effectiveness as they attempt to counsel.

About the only persons who are truly listening to others in our society are psychiatrists, psychologists, and counselors and they are getting paid handsomely for their services. Paid listeners!

A pastor's counsel can be no better than his information. There is only one person who has certain information that the pastor needs and that is the counselee. The only way to receive that information is to hear it. Shakespeare's advice, "Give every man thy ear, but few thy voice," is especially applicable to the pastor-counselor. The pastor who is listening is learning. When a pastor-counselor is talking, the counselee is learning little and the pastor is learning nothing.

Some Africans said of one missionary, "He has soft ears." Soft ears can be one of the major assets of the pastor-counselor. While it is agreed that the pastor must be more than a "big warm ear," he must see the value of listening and he must use accurate listening as the foundation upon which the remainder of his counseling skills rest.

One woman complained to her counselor of her husband, "He does not listen with his heart." All of the "heartless" listening is not being done in parishioners' homes; some of it is being done in pastors' studies. Listening with the heart enables the pastor to hear inaudible cries and to see invisible tears. A pastor's listening skill is not fully developed until he can not only hear what is being said, but also what is not being verbalized.

A common error is to listen faster than the counselee is talking. In doing so the counselor gets ahead of the counselee and begins to draw conclusions upon what he thinks the counselee is going to say. This "you are not with me" awareness is felt by the counselee and he becomes frustrated as he attempts to verbalize his problem.

2. *Responding.* The writer has stated that listening is the foundation upon which all of the counselor's skills rest. One of these skills is that of responding. By properly responding to his verbalizations, the counselee feels that his pastor has truly heard him. This results when the pastor responds to what is said in such a manner as to project that he feels, at least in a measure, as the counselee feels. This feeling is called empathy. Empathy has been defined as, "Your ache in my heart." However, the empathy one feels himself is not

enough; it must be communicated to the counselee. This is the skill of responding.

Responding conveys to the counselee a "Yes, I know how you feel" or a "Yes, I have been there too" feeling. This process of hearing and responding can be most therapeutic for a counselee. This is not to say that all problems are solved by the process of hearing and responding alone; rather, it means that this forms a counselor-counselee bond out of which a helping relationship can grow. Counseling is not so much a meeting of minds as it is a meeting of feelings. The function of counseling is not to let parishioners know where the pastor is; rather, it is to find out where they are. This is achieved primarily through hearing their feelings and responding to them.

3. *Supporting.* Another function of the counselor is that of supporting. The term "support" has many definitions, such as: to sustain, to bear weight or stress, to uphold, or to keep from sinking. All of these definitions are applicable to the supporting role of a pastor. Many persons come to their pastor with a load greater than they feel they can bear. His function is to help his people by sustaining, lifting, upholding, and keeping them from sinking. This does not mean that he assumes the full weight and responsibility of the counselees' problems. Rather, he aids them in bearing the load while they are coming to a better way, through counseling, of dealing with their problems. The dedicated pastor willingly and gladly helps bear these loads because he deeply cares for his people.

4. *Clarifying.* Another function of the counselor is to aid in clarifying the nature of the parishioner's problem. In many cases this clarification is needed because the parishioner has been so close to his problem that he has lost his perspective regarding it. He is so immersed in it that he cannot look at it objectively. Deep problems evoke deep emotions which often obscure from the parishioner that which can be easily seen by the pastor. The parishioner's emotionality adversely affects his rationality. He is propelled by emo-

tion rather than guided by reason. Here the pastor's role is twofold: (1) to reduce emotionality, by letting the parishioner ventilate his feelings; and (2) to increase rationality, by helping him to reality-test his emotional state.

Clarification of the problem must be achieved if there is to be an adequate solution to it. Otherwise the parishioner's attempt at a resolution of the problem will result in his taking an uncertain path toward an undefined destination.

5. *Interpreting.* This is a joint project for the pastor and the parishioner. It involves coming to an understanding of what the problem is, what has caused it, how it has affected the counselee, and what general direction must be taken toward a resolution of it. This is a crucial stage in the counseling process.

6. *Formulating.* This function of the counselor is that of aiding the parishioner in the formulation of a solution to his problem. This process will be twofold: (1) a formulation of attitude, and (2) a formulation of action. A formulation of attitude will involve a new way of evaluating and feeling. A formulation of action will involve a new way of reacting and behaving. There must be a change of attitude before there can be a change in action. Change of attitude is intra-personal in nature while a change of behavior is usually interpersonal in nature.

It should be pointed out that, in the function of formulating, the pastor's role is that of a helper. He must realize that it is the parishioner's problem, not his; therefore the solution to the problem must be formulated by the parishioner with the help of the pastor. Occasionally it may be that the proposed solution to a particular problem is primarily the work of the pastor, but the parishioner must accept it as "his" in the sense that he sees the validity of it and is willing to utilize it. Thus he adopts it and it becomes his own.

The pastor should guard against giving recipe-like solutions to his people's problems. This approach denies the validity of a cooperative approach and tends to make it easy for the pastor to impose plans from the outside rather than letting them emerge from the inside of the counseling relationship.

7. *Guiding*. A last function of the pastor-counselor is that of guiding the parishioner toward his goal, using the road map that was created during the process of formulation. In the early stages of the journey the pastor may need to be quite active in his role as guide. As his parishioner progresses toward his goal, the pastor will become less and less active, so that eventually his help with that particular problem will not be needed at all.

Inasmuch as his ultimate goal for his parishioners is growth, maturity, and wholeness, the pastor-counselor is always seeking to work himself out of a job. That is, so much change is effected in his parishioners that the pastor is not needed in the same way as he was when they were in crisis.

6

The Counseling Interview

THE NATURE OF THE INTERVIEW

The pastor should seek to learn as much information as possible about the counselee and his problem. This is done primarily through the inverview. The interview technique is age-old but a more fundamental and valuable technique is not known.[1] Inasmuch as the major purpose of the counseling interview is to help the counselee develop and carry out better plans for the future, it is important that the pastor realizes that, in effect, he is helping fashion the future of his counselees. Much attention must be given to how he relates himself to the interviewing task, realizing that it will affect future actions of the one he is working with. Paterson, Schneidler, and Williamson state:

> The interview continues to be the most subjective aspect of the diagnostic procedure. Despite its limitations,

however, it is an indispensable step in the guidance program. Its purpose is threefold. It involves gathering all available pertinent facts, making a diagnosis on the basis of all the evidence, and formulating an appropriate plan of action in line with the diagnosis.[2]

The interview, in its most refined state, is akin to art—a developed skill of the interviewer which will be manifested in trained listening, trained watching, and trained talking.

Usually it is better for the pastor to give his counselee a little time to become oriented to the counseling relationship before the problem is vocalized. This can be achieved by beginning the interview with a reference to the outcome of a recent ball game, by making an observation regarding the weather, or by referring to a known interest or hobby of the parishioner. This element of the interview should not consume too much time; so after the topic opener has been given cursory attention, the interview should move easily and naturally into the problem which is confronting the counselee.

The beginning pastor-counselor must be cautioned not to assume that the presenting problem (the initial statement of the problem) is the *real* problem or that it is *all* of the problem. Sometimes the presenting problem is used by the counselee to test the counselor. In these cases it may be a deliberate attempt to see how the pastor will react, or it may be an attempt on the part of the parishioner to see how the pastor will respond to him. Sometimes the presenting problem is a deliberate attempt to conceal a deeper problem from the pastor. However, in most cases it is not deliberate but unconscious.

The pastor needs to be aware of the fact that the presenting problem may be much like an iceberg which has one-seventh exposed and six-sevenths which cannot be seen. If the pastor attacks the presenting problem immediately, it is quite likely that the full problem will never be confronted. This being so, the parishioner will leave still frustrated, and the pastor will be led to the false assumption that he has solved the parishioner's problem.

It is important to give the counselee the time he needs. This will permit him a free expression of the problem and, in the process, provide a needed emotional release. If a fluid expression is permitted the counselee, he will sense that the pastor is not forcing him. This also helps him to feel that he can trust him. If he is hurried or forced, the counselee is apt to "close up" and the problem will not only be unsolved; it will be deepened. If the counselee falls into a period of silence, the pastor should not be alarmed or disturbed at the lack of apparent progress. Many writers have stated that this silence can be a means of forcing the problem to the surface. Therefore periods of silence, and the moments immediately following them, may be the most significant parts of the interview.

Once the problem has been adequately stated and both are convinced that it is the *real* problem, they can work together toward a solution. A basic skill needed by the counselor is the ability to ask pertinent and meaningful questions, the answers to which will give insight into the problem of the counselee. The interview must have a goal. "If much is to be accomplished, a clarification of objectives must be made or the interview may lapse into a period of pointless conversation."[3]

Toward the end of the interview, it is desirable and necessary to summarize the development made. This summarization should be initiated and directed by the pastor but actually done by the counselee. This tends to add clarity to both what has been done and what remains to be done.

Shostrom and Brammer feel that the most important part of the interview is the *synthesizing phase*.[4] This phase is that which crystallizes all of the information received in the interview into a definite plan of action. Erickson concurs, feeling that the counselee should leave with some plans for action and with some resolve to implement these plans through a program of doing.[5] The counselee should leave with a feeling of satisfaction, knowing that he has been aided by his counselor both to objectify his problem and to find a solution for it.

Erickson conceives the interview technique to be a highly skilled professional service.[6] Such skill is achieved only by careful study and much experience. The pastor will need to develop flexibility. As people differ, so must the interview techniques differ. The counselor who develops this quality of adaptation will have mastered his key problem in successful interviewing.

Hahn and MacLean say: "Old as the interview is in professional history, it has been subjected to relatively little research of a crucial type."[7] With continued development in the research and methodology of interviewing, it may well be that this information will open up hitherto unknown and unexplored areas in counseling which will immeasurably aid the pastor as he engages in the counseling function of the ministry.

THE SETTING FOR COUNSELING

Though the setting for counseling is an important matter, it is not a crucial one. Much has been written about the ideal setting, leaving the reader with the impression that if the ideal cannot be attained the counseling relationship cannot be effective. While the ideal is desirable, it is certainly not necessary. There are two prime factors to be kept in mind: (1) there should be a maximum of privacy, and (2) there should be a minimum of interruption. "Maximum of privacy" means that the matters being discussed are being heard by only the counselor and the counselee. A "minimum of interruption" means that the counseling process should proceed without being broken by intrusions which make it difficult for the counselee to talk freely and for the counselor to listen well.

It is possible for a counseling relationship to be established in a number of settings, such as the pastor's study, elsewhere in the church building, in the home of the parishioner, in the parsonage, in an automobile, in a restaurant, or on an outing.

1. *In the study*. With the above two considerations in mind, it is most likely that the best setting for counseling will be in the pastor's study. While there is no guarantee that the pastor's study will offer a maximum of privacy and a minimum of interruption, the possibility of meeting these two criteria is greater there than anywhere else because the control factor is greater. If a visitor knocks at the study door, the pastor can either dispose of the matter of business in a few seconds or, if not, he can simply say, "I am in conference at the moment. Could we talk about this at a later time?" Likewise, if his phone rings during the counseling interview, he can quickly handle that interruption in the same manner. Fortunate is the pastor who has a secretary who can intercept both visitors and phone calls, so that the counseling process can proceed in complete privacy without interruption.

2. *In the church*. Pastoral counseling can be done in the church itself, but there is always the possibility of being interrupted by a teacher coming to arrange his room for next Sunday's lesson, an organist or pianist coming to practice, a janitor making his rounds, or a deliveryman bringing supplies to the church. Also, the parishioner has the feeling that persons other than the pastor may be hearing him, inasmuch as he is in a public building that is open to anyone at any time.

3. *In the home*. Pastoral counseling can be done in the home of the parishioner, but again the possibilities for nonprivacy and interruptions are great. At any moment other members of the home may arrive, the phone may ring, a neighbor might visit, or a salesman might call at the door. Where small children are present it becomes extremely difficult for a counseling relationship to continue without interruption.

4. *In the parsonage*. The parsonage offers a possible setting for a counseling interview but many persons are

reluctant to go there, particularly women, because they feel they are entering another woman's private domain. Also, if the matter being discussed is to be known by the pastor alone, the parishioner may not feel free to "open up," even if members of the pastor's family are not in the room but in other areas of the home.

5. *In an automobile.* Counseling can be done in an automobile but it does not offer the optimum setting for a good counseling relationship. The exposure is great and the possibilities for interruptions are enormous. Then too, this setting for counseling is open only to members of the pastor's own sex inasmuch as it otherwise would create suspicion, casting a reflection on the character of both pastor and parishioner.

6. *In a restaurant.* Pastoral counseling can be done in a restaurant, or other public building, but there are distinct disadvantages in doing so for the reasons mentioned above.

7. *On an outing.* Much is to be said in favor of engaging in pastoral counseling when a pastor is on a fishing or hunting trip or some other kind of outing with one of his men or boys. Usually the counseling can proceed at a leisurely pace under the conditions of both privacy and intimacy. Wise is the pastor who can turn such a leisure-time activity into a genuine helping relationship for his parishioner.

PHYSICAL FACTORS

Assuming that a pastor will elect to do most of his counseling in his study, he can do much, at little cost, to make the counseling setting a pleasant one. If the pastor has a voice in the construction and layout of the study, several matters should receive his consideration: (1) the study door should be hung so that, when opened, it does not expose his counselee to visitors at the door; (2) the room should be made as soundproof as possible (carpeting and drapes help); (3) it should be neither too large nor too small; (4) it should be arranged so that the pastor can be seated in a place other than behind his desk while counseling; (5) the chairs should be placed so that neither the pastor nor the parishioner faces the glaring daylight; (6) the lighting should be somewhat subdued and arranged so that neither the pastor nor the parishioner must look directly into it; and (7) the study should have an outside entrance easily identifiable and accessible from the street. If the church has a secretary and a secretary's office, her office should be placed in a manner so that it can be a reception room for the pastor's study.

The pastor should give attention to the chairs in which his counselees will be seated. They should be comfortable, preferably with arms, and somewhat erect and rigid.

The study should be kept neat and clean. The pastor's desk should be kept reasonably free of papers, letters, and books so that the parishioner does not feel that he is interrupting the "work" of the pastor. (Counseling is as much his work as anything else he does.) In short, the study should be well-arranged and well-appointed and the pastor's attention and attitude should be such as to suggest to the parishioner that he is welcome there and that he has a "right" to a counseling interview.

PSYCHOLOGICAL FACTORS

If rapport in the counseling situation is to be achieved, a pastor must be aware of the psychological factors present in the counseling relationship. The pastor should remember that in many cases the counselee comes with timidity. This may be the result of natural personality characteristics, apprehension, or the lack of information of "what will happen to him" or "what the pastor will do to him." It may be simply a matter of embarrassment, due to the fact that his very presence before the pastor testifies of his inadequacy to cope with his problem. These elements should show the pastor the necessity for creating relaxed and friendly conditions which will tend to reduce tension, apprehension, and anxiety in the parishioner.

When any two people meet for the first time, they formulate certain opinions of one another that are altered or substantiated in later contacts. If, in the initial meeting, adverse opinions are formed by the counselee, the counseling process is slowed down until a working relationship is established. It behooves the interviewer to take stock of himself at the beginning of each interview so that a minimum number of opinion obstacles will be present.[8]

The parishioner should receive the impression that his problem is the most important task, and the only task, of the counselor at the moment. This will do much to help him enter into a wholesome interchange of thoughts and ideas. Hahn and MacLean see the establishment of rapport as a joint responsibility of the counselee and the counselor. They say:

> On the part of the counselee it involves developing a feeling of ease, born of growing confidence in the counselor's competence, interest, knowledge, and skill, and a feeling of freedom to reveal both facts and emotions. On the part of the counselor it entails treating a counselee as a responsible adult, being considerate of all attitudes and feelings.[9]

Most pastors will not find it necessary to take notes during the counseling session. While this is done regularly in a clinic or counseling center, it is not recommended for most pastoral counselors. This is so for several reasons; namely, (1) most pastors know their people and their problems so well that it is not necessary to take notes; (2) some parishioners do not want the intimate aspects of their lives preserved in written form by their pastors; and (3) note-taking can be distracting to both the pastor and the parishioner. However, if the pastor's counseling load is so heavy, or his memory is so poor, that he feels it is necessary to take notes during the interview, he should do so openly without attempting to conceal it from his counselee.

In most cases a pastor can record any necessary notes after the interview, thus escaping the negative aspects of note-taking listed above. When notes are taken of an interview, they should be carefully preserved by the pastor, making sure that he is the only one who will ever have access to them, except on written approval for their release by the person involved.

What has been said regarding note-taking can also be said for tape recordings of interviews. Most pastors will find it neither necessary nor desirable to preserve their interviews on tape. However, if it is done, it should be done only with the knowledge and consent of the parishioner, and great care should be taken to insure the anonymity and privacy of the individual.

While the counseling setting is important, it must be fully understood that the most important matter is the counseling relationship. If the relationship between the pastor and the parishioner is strong and positive, a fruitful counseling session can be conducted even under the most adverse circumstances. Conversely, if the relationship is not characterized by openness, warmth, and trust, little value is likely to result even if the counseling takes place in the most ideal of settings. While a pastor may not be able to do his counseling under ideal conditions, he can always create a climate of caring, and this is the setting that matters most.

What Is Not Known About Counseling

While there are many things that we do know about counseling, there are some things that we do not know. Here are some of these issues:

1. It is not known exactly what it is that helps the person to resolve his problems. Certainly it is not the technique that a counselor uses. As one looks into the literature of counseling and learns the various styles and techniques that are employed, it can be seen that there is a wide range in methods. The best assumption is that the reason a person is helped is because of the relationship that he establishes with the counselor. Most of the literature that one reads will af-

firm this, but it should be pointed out that this cannot be scientifically established.

2. It is not known why a person changes. It is probably because his hurt forces him to seek an existence that is characterized by less pain and more pleasure. It would seem that this is a valid assumption, yet it is a guess at best.

3. It is not known how a person changes. Is there some kind of mechanism for change which a person has resident in him? If so, does he have some kind of awareness of how to engage this mechanism for change so that the processes for change can be set in motion? Again, there is no answer to this.

4. It is not known whether to approach a given case primarily through a modification of behavior or through a modification of environment. While in most cases there will need to be a change in both, the problem is to know which of these should be pursued first and which area should receive the greater amount of attention during the counseling process.

5. It is not known in advance how directive or nondirective the counselor should be in any given case. The literature of the field suggests that younger persons, less mature persons, and less knowledgeable persons will usually be helped better by a more direct approach in counseling, whereas older, mature, and more educated persons will likely respond better to the nondirective approach. However, every experienced counselor knows that this theory does not always hold. This means, then, that relationship precedes technique and that the counseling session itself will dictate what is the best technique with any given person at any given time.

6. It is not known whether there is a direct correlation between the amount and type of the counselor's training and his success in counseling. Of course, it is assumed that there is such a direct correlation and this book has even suggested that such a correlation exists. However, there is no real way of proving that such is so. Studies have shown that enormous success has been achieved by what is known as "lay counselors" whose training is short-term.

Because there is so much that is not known about counseling, the enterprise should be approached with a great deal of modesty. Preconceived notions should be held lightly, and one must be willing at any time to discard them when valid evidence shows that they are not correct.

Don'ts for the Pastor-Counselor

1. Don't hurry the counselee.

2. Don't immediately ask for clarification at some point if the counselee is verbalizing freely. This can be clarified later.

3. Don't assume that reason is stronger than emotions to a person who is in crisis.

4. Don't seek for information that is not needed or will not be used.

5. Don't be shocked by any problem that is presented to you.

6. Don't try to prove to a counselee that he is right or wrong.

7. Don't attempt to *force* moral-ethical values upon the counselee.

8. Don't assume that you know the solution to every problem that is brought to you.

9. Don't assume that you are *supposed* to know the solution to every problem that is brought to you.

10. Don't be reluctant to refer the counselee to a professional counselor if you cannot help him.

Do's for the Pastor-Counselor

1. Do remember that the counselee has offered you an invitation to intimacy which requires that his problem must be approached with as much care and competency as you can bring to it.

2. Do recognize that his confidence must never be betrayed.

3. Do be understanding, compassionate, concerned.
4. Do listen much and talk little.
5. Do be aware of what is, and is not, being said.
6. Do remember that his frustration has caused a subjectivity which must be diluted by your objectivity.
7. Do believe that the counselee is normal until you are convinced otherwise.
8. Do believe in your ability to help until it is proved otherwise.
9. Do look for distorted concepts of God.
10. Do keep a biblical view of man in mind.
11. Do be aware of the divine resources upon which both you and your counselee can draw.

7

Premarital Counseling

We can no longer assume, as we naively have in the past, that *wanting* to be married constitutes the major qualification for success in marriage. How foolish to think that marriage, the most complex of all interpersonal relationships, can be successful simply because two people are in love and wish to live their lives together!

It seems that our society, including the Church, has chosen to ignore the staggering facts of what is happening to the institution of marriage in our times. There is no need to quote the dismal statistics regarding the number of divorces and separations that are occurring daily. It is necessary for us only to admit to what exists and we will be brought quickly to the position that something must be done to halt the momentum of the increasing meaninglessness of marriage that is threatening to crush our society.

Social scientists have been trying to tell us for decades that we have not taken preparation for marriage seriously. Their message has largely been ignored until fairly recent times. Slowly we are beginning to hear what they have been telling us and, as a society, we are making some feeble efforts toward better preparation of persons for marriage.

As a whole, the Church does not have a record in this area of which she can be proud. The time has come for the Church to cease feeling that she has done her part by providing a staff (pastor, musicians, and others) who can take part in the marriage ceremony, and the facilities in which the wedding and reception can take place. The Church must take preparation for marriage seriously and inaugurate ways and means of helping persons approach marriage in a manner that will increase the possibility for success.

QUESTIONS TO BE ANSWERED

The pastor sometimes has to answer some moral-ethical questions regarding the proposed marriages of certain persons. As he engages in premarital counseling with persons previously unknown to him, he will encounter some situations that will cause him to think deeply and pray earnestly concerning whether he should perform certain marriages. Some of these moral-ethical decisions are related to such questions as: (1) Should he marry non-Christians? (2) Should he marry a Christian and a non-Christian? (3) Should he marry persons of widely divergent faiths? (4) Should he marry underage persons whose marriage is not fully endorsed by the parents of both? (5) Should he marry divorced persons? (6) Should he marry persons with obvious mental deficiency? (7) Should he marry persons of different races? and (8) Should he marry persons he has not counseled?

Granted, some of these questions are not moral-ethical *per se*, but moral-ethical implications can arise out of them. Each pastor will have to make his own decisions in the light of his own conscience and reason as well as the guidance he receives from the Holy Spirit and the Bible, and, in a measure, by the directives of his own denomination.

Differences in Marital and Premarital Counseling

While there are many similarities between counseling the married and counseling the unmarried, there are also some marked differences. Some of these differences are:

1. *Premarital counseling is usually initiated by the pastor, whereas marital counseling is usually initiated by the parishioner.* Some authorities question whether premarital counseling should be called "counseling" at all, inasmuch as one of the major elements of counseling is not present, namely, a felt need on the part of the counselee. Most persons who come for premarital counseling do not have a "felt need." In fact, most of them are in such a blissful state that the idea of hurt is foreign to their thinking. The pastor should be aware that such an attitude will militate against the effectiveness of his counseling work. Many couples will view premarital counseling as something to "get out of the way" so that plans for the wedding can be finalized. This attitude should not deter the pastor from doing this necessary work. It is vitally important, even though it is not viewed as being so by many of his counselees.

2. *Premarital counseling emphasizes the cognitive aspect, whereas marital counseling emphasizes the affective dimension.* Because most persons who come for premarital counseling are not hurting (as persons in marital crisis are), it naturally follows that the counseling sessions center largely in the cognitive-rational area. In a marital crisis the affective (feelings, emotions) militates against the cognitive (perceiving, knowing); therefore change in feeling must precede change in thinking. In premarital counseling the negative affective dimension is usually not present, which means that

the sessions can proceed on a more rational, matter-of-fact basis.

3. *Premarital counseling employs the directive method more than is normally used in marital counseling.* When the pastor counsels the unmarried, he takes a very active part in the process. He has certain goals he wishes to accomplish and he has definite methods he employs to reach those goals. He does much of the talking. In premarital situations he *presents* a program, whereas he lets it *emerge* when he is engaged in marital counseling. In premarital counseling the pastor is first of all a teacher (an information giver); in marital counseling he is at first a learner (an information receiver).

GOALS FOR PREMARITAL COUNSELING

The pastor must have both general and specific goals he seeks for his counselees to achieve in premarital counseling. The general goals include the following: (1) an understanding of the meaning of marriage within the framework of biblical truth and Christian theology, (2) an understanding of the problems affecting marriage in contemporary culture, and (3) an understanding of the Christian concept of the value of human personality. As the pastor deals with these broad concepts he seeks to expand his counselees' awareness of the importance of marriage in the light of its biblical and historical roots, of the unique pressures being brought upon marriage in our times, and of Christianity's view of the worth of persons. All of these goals are of vital importance in building a sound philosophy of marriage.

The specific goals center in the following areas: (1) an understanding of each partner's role-perception in the forthcoming marriage, (2) an understanding of each partner's role-expectation of the other, (3) an understanding of how each partner evaluates the strengths and weaknesses of the other, (4) an understanding of the potential strengths and weaknesses of the proposed marriage, and (5) a careful examination of particular problems likely to arise.

The underlying, practical goal of all premarital counseling is twofold: (1) to enable the partners to pre-solve some potential marriage problems before they arise; and (2) to give the partners knowledge of, and experience in, the art of communication, which is so necessary in the building of a rich and rewarding relationship.

THE VALUES OF PREMARITAL COUNSELING

There are many values in premarital counseling if it is done carefully and consistently by the pastor. One of these values is the satisfaction that it brings to him personally. He feels he has done something to elevate the institution of marriage in a society that is taking a casual, if not careless, attitude toward it. True, no one pastor can change this societal attitude by himself, but each one can experience the inner reward of knowing he has done his part to change this prevailing attitude. He also has the satisfaction of knowing that he has played a vital part in helping the couples he works with to establish their marriages on a stronger foundation than they would be able to otherwise.

The values of premarital counseling accruing to the prospective marriage partners are many. One of these values is the acquisition of a better view of the nature of the institution of marriage and of the meaning of marriage within the Christian tradition. Unfortunately, many persons who approach marriage have not taken the time to study the significance of the marriage relationship nor have they seriously evaluated the demands that marriage will place upon them. As noted before most young couples are aware of only two things: (1) they are in love, and (2) they want to spend their lives together. While these two aspects must be present if a marriage is to succeed, success will not be guaranteed by these factors alone. Thinking through the implications of marriage with a third party will enable the couple to approach marriage more realistically.

Another value of premarital counseling is that it affords

each partner a better understanding of himself. This results when the pastor helps each to evaluate his own personality in terms of motives, attitudes, and disposition. If done thoroughly, premarital counseling can be a process of self-revelation to one as his pastor helps him confront himself at the deepest levels of his own being. While this process can be somewhat painful, it need not be threatening if the individual is aware that his pastor is truly concerned about him, his partner, and their future relationship.

A value of great importance is the knowledge that each partner gains of the other through the counseling process. The pastor must help the partners to gain a greater understanding of the thought patterns of each other. They will be surprised to find out how little each really knows about the other. Some couples feel that knowing each other includes only the basic biographical data about each. But the perimeter of person· hood goes much beyond this factual information. It is possible to know all *about* a person without *knowing* him. In fact, the greater dimensions of personhood lie largely beyond the boundaries of biographical data. Through the skillful, but gentle, probing of the pastor, the partners begin to gain a greater clarity of each other's boundary of being.

Another practical value of premarital counseling is that partners can see the value of, and gain experience in, the skill of communication. This is the skill that both must develop if the marriage is to survive, let alone thrive.

Still another value to be considered is that the couple is afforded a more valid means of evaluating their forthcoming marriage. In many cases, couples forecast their future on the basis of incomplete, if not inaccurate, data. By helping the partners to expand their fund of knowledge of each other and of the marriage relationship, the pastor aids them in establishing a better basis on which to forecast the marriage.

Finally, a great value of premarital counseling is that it helps persons to realistically determine if they are making the right choice regarding marriage. Some may think that premarital counseling comes too late in a relationship to prevent an unfortunate marriage from occurring. Nevertheless, it does happen on some occasions. The result is a two-stage process: (1) postponing the wedding, and then (2) cancelling the marriage.

While it is not the job of the pastor to talk persons out of marriage, it is his duty to help them thoroughly examine their readiness for marriage. If, through his expert and gentle help, persons come to see that they do not have an adequate basis for establishing a marriage, the pastor has saved them an enormous amount of pain and anxiety.

Through the process of talking with an understanding counselor, a person may discover that repressed fears regarding his partner begin to emerge. He begins to see that partner more objectively. One young woman, who later decided not to enter marriage, found that, through the process of talking, some fears regarding her fiancé began to "surface." Note the insights to which she came:

"He's not a 'people' person [she was]; he's a 'thing' person."

"It scares me because he's so unpredictable."

"He's so independent he may not need me."

While it cannot be said that she would not have come to these insights without counseling, in all probability the counseling process helped her to see what she would not have seen otherwise and to reverse her course in time.

LIMITATIONS OF PREMARITAL COUNSELING

While there are many values of premarital counseling, it is only fair to mention some of its limitations. One of the most serious limitations is that many persons are so blinded by love (or what they assume to be love) that they cannot enter into premarital counseling with any degree of objectivity. Persons who are caught in this "mild psychosis" are not likely to be helped greatly, regardless of the degree of skill of the pastor-counselor.

The two factors of time and timing may seriously affect the value of premarital counseling in any given situation. The pastor may not have the amount of time he needs to adequately counsel the unmarried. This may be because of his own work load at the time or because the persons involved do not allow him enough time to counsel with them adequately before the proposed wedding. Timing is another important matter. Timing has to do with the point in the relationship at which the pastor enters the picture as the counselor. If the date has been set, the invitations mailed, and the out-of-town relatives are en route to the wedding, it is not likely that any in-depth work can be done by the pastor! Certainly, it is most unlikely that a cancellation of the wedding would occur under such circumstances even if one or both parties have serious reservations about the marriage. Hopefully, the timing for premarital counseling should be early enough so that in-depth work can be accomplished under the most ideal of circumstances.

Another limitation of premarital counseling is that it is of little value to persons who are extremely immature. (Immaturity is not gauged by years. Persons are young once but they may be immature a lifetime.) Such people are incapable of approaching marriage (or anything else) objectively. Potential problems that are presented to them are quickly dismissed with a "we can work that out" attitude and response. (A sensitive pastor may need to determine if he wishes to endorse a wedding, by his participation, where the two parties evidence a great amount of immaturity.)

METHOD OF PROCEDURE

The pastor who wishes to do a creditable job of premarital counseling should think in terms of at least three sessions: (1) one with the woman, (2) one with the man, and (3) one with both. In each of the individual sessions the pastor will be engaging in four main functions: (1) listening, (2) questioning, (3) analyzing, and (4) teaching.

1. *Listening.* As in other types of counseling, the pastor needs to hear what is, and is not, being said. Only by careful listening can the pastor come to valid insights regarding the counselee's real feelings about his personal relationship with the proposed marriage partner. Though the pastor will probably do much of the talking in this situation, it is imperative that when he does listen he does so with such skill that he will gather adequate and accurate data. This he will later use as he engages in the function of analyzing.

2. *Questioning.* Skillful use of questions enables the pastor to gather the type of data he needs to help persons prepare for marriage. Questioning will center in the two broad areas of facts and feelings. The area of facts will have to do with such aspects as how they met, how long they have known each other, how long they have dated, and when they plan to marry. The questioning should then move to the deeper level of feelings. This area has to do with such matters as the counselee's true feelings about the idea of marriage, the demands of marriage, his perception of his partner as a marriage mate, and his own feelings regarding his ability to be a suitable marriage partner.

The pastor should not hesitate to question his counselees regarding their feelings about every aspect of the marriage relationship including such matters as where they will live and in what kind of dwelling, how many children they want, where they will attend church, whether the wife will be employed outside the home (along with how long, how much, and what kind of work), how they will use their leisure time, where they will find their friends and how they will develop social relationships, how each feels about the husband's job, and if either plans for further education. He should also examine their attitudes toward in-laws, money, and sex. As the pastor probes the deeper levels of his parishioners' feelings he gains the type and amount of information he needs as he proceeds to analysis.

3. *Analyzing.* After the data is sorted out and analyzed,

the pastor is ready for a joint session (or sessions) with the partners. In most cases there will be some differences in how each partner perceives certain aspects of the future marriage. These are the areas that will need to be given special and careful attention during the joint session. It is at this time that the two partners will need to be shown the importance of communication. It will also provide a rich opportunity for them to begin to develop new and better ways of communicating their feelings to each other.

4. *Teaching*. Lastly, the pastor engages in the function of teaching. The amount and type of teaching that is to be done will be determined by what the pastor has discovered in the individual counseling sessions. The broad areas covered in his teaching will usually include the Christian view of marriage, the status of marriage in contemporary culture, the responsible use of sex, the basic differences in maleness and femaleness (most feel they understand the opposite sex but do not), and the art of communication. As a part of his teaching function the pastor should be prepared to recommend and loan helpful books and articles in areas where the partners lack understanding. It is also important for the pastor to point out the value of a medical examination for the prospective bride, if not for both partners.

Conclusion

Thorough work in premarital counseling may involve more than three counseling sessions, but that is the minimum. While this is both time-consuming and exhausting, it is less so than marriage counseling. If a pastor does his premarital counseling work well he may be saving himself, or some other pastor or counselor, from involvement in more extensive marriage counseling later on. Of greater significance, of course, is that premarital counseling helps couples to build the kind of relationships that are both solid and satisfying.

8

Marriage Counseling

The contemporary pastor is called upon for various types of counseling: religious, personal-social, vocational, educational, premarital, and marital. Many beginning ministers find it most disturbing to learn that the type of counseling for which they are best prepared—religious—is not the type of counseling they are called upon to do most frequently. They will probably find that they are sought more for marriage and family counseling than for any other type. But this is disturbing to them because their educational experiences have not equipped them to minister effectively as counselors in these areas. Not a few will wish they had majored in psychology or sociology in college, and even those who did will wish they had listened better and studied more! Often the lament is heard by their college and seminary mentors, "I never dreamed that people could have so many problems and that their problems could be so complex. I need help!"

This chapter will deal with some of the major aspects of this kind of counseling. It is hoped that it will afford the reader some insights and information as he deals with this difficult, though rewarding, kind of counseling.

SOCIETAL PRESSURES ON MARRIAGE

Marriage is the most complex of all interpersonal relationships. This is true because the affective dimension of personality is involved more in marriage than in other kinds of relationships. It is no simple matter for two separate and distinct personalities to blend together as one while still maintaining the identity of each. Attempting to do so in a society which, by its very nature and values, brings enormous pressures on the marriage relationship further complicates the problem. These outside forces have a way of getting inside the marriage relationship, thus compounding an already complex and delicate situation. Some of these societal pressures on marriage are as follows:

1. *The erosion of moral values.* There is no longer a universal, clear-cut definition for morality. We have come to a period like that of the judges, when "every man did that which was right in his own eyes" (Judg. 21:25). To millions of persons in contemporary society, matters such as adultery, homosexuality, abortion, and divorce are purely personal evaluations as far as their rightness or wrongness is concerned. To them there are no external, universal standards governing conduct.

2. *The importance placed upon materialism.* Peter Marshall called materialism "the hook that is baited with security." Emerson said, "The trouble with money is that it costs too much." Part of that cost is the loss of the life of a marriage which desperately but unsuccessfully tries to pay for what it cannot afford. The search for security and the desire

for things can cause persons to give their attention to, and place values on, matters that can destroy the marriage relationship rather than build it. Marriage should be approached qualitatively, not quantitatively.

3. *The role confusion of husband and wife.* This results because there is no longer a clear-cut distinction between man's work and woman's work. In millions of homes there are now two breadwinners instead of one. This means that what once was clearly the work (and therefore the authority and responsibility) of one has become the shared task of both. This results in the couple's not knowing the true role of each partner and the children's not knowing the true role of both parents.

4. *The value placed upon youth and charm.* The American home is being bombarded continuously through the mass media by society's twin ideals of youthfulness and attractiveness. The message that comes through is that the old (over 30) and ugly (less than handsome or beautiful) are undesirable. We are deluged by this through newspapers, magazines, billboards, radio, and television and it is affecting American marriages more than is realized.

FUNCTIONS OF THE MARRIAGE COUNSELOR

1. The first function of the marriage counselor is to hear the hurts that the counselees are feeling. In many cases these hurts have been intense, of long duration, and unexpressed to a third party. The reason that the counselor needs to hear the hurts is because the counselee feels his partner has not truly heard him. Attempts to be heard by his mate have been aborted, and this adds to his anxiety and frustration. When he feels that his counselor is getting his message and is feeling with him, he experiences the catharsis he needs in order to approach his problem more realistically.

2. Another function of marriage counseling is to clarify problems. Most persons who come for counsel are aware of symptoms but they do not understand what is producing

those symptoms. As one distraught married woman put it, "My problem is I don't know what my problem is." Through the counseling process she came to see both her marital problem and why it had developed.

3. A third function is to help in the understanding of roles. In many cases of marital crisis, there is a gap between role-perception and role-performance and there is also a gap between role-expectation and role-performance. The gap between role-perception and role-performance is the difference between the way one views himself and the manner in which he behaves. The gap between role-expectation and role-performance is the difference between how one thinks his partner should behave and how he actually behaves. Because it is difficult for one to see the gap between his perception of himself and his behavior, he feels that he is misunderstood if his mate points out this discrepancy to him. When both partners are thus criticizing each other, each feels mistreated and frustrated.

4. A fourth function of the marriage counselor is to facilitate communication. Inasmuch as the subject of communication will be discussed later in this chapter, it will not be dealt with at this point except to say that at the base of most marital discord there is a problem of communication.

5. A fifth function is to encourage change in perception and behavior. It is not enough for the counselor to hear hurts, clarify problems, aid in the understanding of roles, and aid in facilitating communication. He must help motivate the partners both to think themselves into a new way of behaving and to behave themselves into a new way of thinking. Motivation is usually achieved, at least to a degree, when feelings have been ventilated, the problem is seen in clearer perspective, and communication lines have been opened.

THE WAR AND THE BATTLEGROUND

Marriage, which begins as a conspiracy to conquer isolation and loneliness through mutual surrender, often deteriorates into an open warfare. In marital conflict it is important for the counselor to distinguish the war from the battlegound. Many things—sex, money, in-laws, discipline of children—can become battlegrounds but these may not in themselves represent the basis for the conflict. They may be the occasions, but not the causes, for marital conflict. The *why* of a battle must be separated from the *where* of the battle. In World War II some of the fiercest battles were fought on islands which were of little value in themselves. The opposing forces were fighting on, but not really for, those islands. The same is often the case in marital conflict.

Most couples are not aware of the difference between the basic conflict and the immediate source of tension. As long as these are confused it is not likely that there will be any healing in the relationship. One of the major tasks of the pastor is to help the two partners understand *why* there is a conflict. As long as the couple and the counselor are surveying the battleground it is not likely that they will come to understand the reasons for the war. The reasons for a marital war may be limited, but the battlegrounds on which to fight it seem to be limitless.

The Problem of Communication

The greatest cause for marital conflict is lack of communication. Over and over the marriage counselor hears this theme-song from his counselees—"We can't talk with each other." There are many stanzas in this theme-song, such as:

"She never tells me what she's thinking."

"He never lets me know how he feels."

"I can't figure her out—I don't really know her."

"All I get from him is silence."

"We don't understand each other."

Effective communication involves both the sending and receiving of messages. But communication in marriage must be deeper; it must also be the sending and receiving of feelings. In other words, communication must be both rational and emotional. When communication involves both facts and feelings it facilitates understanding between two persons. Accurate communication serves two basic functions: (1) it discloses the "location" of both persons, and (2) it facilitates adjustment by revealing the gap between them.

There is always a gap between any two persons who have entered a relationship. The gap is best narrowed when both persons determine to do so. This is called "adjustment." The gap can be narrowed less effectively when only one party determines to do so. This is called "compliance."

Compliance is often only rational in nature. Because it is not both rational *and* emotional, it is often short-lived; or if it endures, it does so at the cost of a degree of personhood by the complier. One feels he is playing a role and his heart is not in it. It is like attempting one-handed applause; it is silently frustrating.

Compliance, however virtuous, cannot be a substitute for adjustment. Adjustment is achieved when both parties see the gap (because they have been truly communicating), both see the reason for the gap, both desire that the gap be narrowed, and each willingly and deliberately begins to move in the direction of the other. Thus the elements of adjustment are twofold: rational (seeing the need to adjust) and affective (wanting to adjust).

The following describes the nature of a communication-less marriage: Visualize a couple in a huge gymnasium on a dark night with the lights out, each in stocking feet and each with a gag in the mouth. Conceivably, these people could spend the entire night trying to find each other, only to fail in the process. Or if they "find" each other, it might be the result of a painful collision. Some marriages are operated on this basis. The result is frustration and anguish.

Continuing with the illustration, communication "turns on the light," revealing the exact location of each, thus revealing the direction each must go for them to get together. Healthy communication not only discloses the direction each must go; it also determines a reasonable distance each should travel in order to get together. The maxim, "Marriage is a 50-50 proposition," is beautiful theoretically but faulty operationally. At times marriage will be a 100-0, a 90-10, a 20-80, or a 40-60 proposition. Persons in an open, trusting relationship have no need to compile direction-distance statistics.

The dual emotional needs of loving and needing to be loved are much like inhaling and exhaling. Just as physical life cannot be sustained by either inhaling or exhaling, so emotional life cannot be sustained by either loving or needing to be loved. The mutual process of sending and receiving positive feelings (loving and needing to be loved) builds strong persons and a strong marriage. The amount of verbiage is not the important factor in communication; what matters is the nature and quality of the self-revelation.

Communication problems may take various forms: (1) faulty communication, (2) negative communication, (3) deceptive communication, (4) one-level communication, or (5) non-communication (silence).

1. Faulty communication may result from either garbled talking or garbled hearing. Sometimes it is the result of both. One counselee told his counselor, "My wife and I can't communicate. We send messages but they are not heard accurately." He was half right; neither were they talking accurately. This dual communication problem brought their marriage to a crisis and brought them to a counselor. Another couple, whose surface problem was financial due to the stress of trying to make $160 house payments on a monthly income of $360, arrived at a crisis because of inaccurate communication. Neither wanted to buy the house but each thought the other did. Illustrations of this kind of problem in communication are legion.

2. A serious form of communication problem is negative communication. This means that talking is designed to

hurt or destroy the other partner. Sometimes words are used as chisels to chip away at the personhood of another. Being hurt causes a desire to retaliate. It thus becomes a self-defeating syndrome. This style of communication is extremely difficult to change and, in many cases, it brings the relationship to a degree of crisis from which it may never recover. Usually a change in this style of communicating involves a change in motivation, a feat which is most difficult to accomplish even under the guidance of a skilled counselor.

3. Deceptive communication is a deliberate attempt to hide true feelings with untrue words; for example, verbalizing love when there is no love. Persons engaging in this form of communication may do so for various reasons, such as: (1) fear of hurting the other, (2) fear of facing the problems that result from openness, or (3) desire to keep a marriage intact while engaging in an illicit relationship. Not all communication reveals; sometimes it conceals. This form of communication problem is one of the most serious because it provides the partner inaccurate data with which to work. When the truth is revealed, it is devastating because trust, the cement of a relationship, disintegrates and the marriage shatters.

4. One-level communication deals only with surface matters of an impersonal nature. This is the type of communication problem that is present in many, if not most, marriages. Couples may engage in a great amount of conversation but their talk never reveals how they truly feel, particularly about each other. A counselor said to a couple as they were leaving his office, "You may get to know each other yet." When they returned the next week the wife said, "I've thought all week about what you told us last week when we were leaving. I realize that you are right—we really haven't known each other." Their 10-year marriage had been characterized by a lot of talking which had said nothing. Their one-level communication had centered in the external and impersonal. The deeper level of communication deals with matters of an in-

ternal, personal nature. Through this latter kind one discloses (exposes) himself to another by revealing feelings. The pastor will need to show his counselees how to engage in a deeper level of communication.

5. Non-communication (silence) is a form of communication which may be either passive or aggressive. The silence of non-communication may "say" many things: (1) "I cannot talk to you"; (2) "I am afraid to talk to you"; or (3) "I will not talk to you." All of these are unhealthy. Couples who are not talking are living in solitary confinement together. They are living together separately. They may live under the same roof, sleep in the same bed, and eat at the same table, but theirs is only a geographical togetherness. As the layers of accumulated silence build higher between them, they know each other less and dislike each other more. On the wall of a certain counselor's office is a poster which reads, "People are lonely because they build walls instead of bridges." Silence is an expert in building walls; it knows nothing of building bridges.

The greatest service a pastor can render to persons in marital conflict is to aid them in the process of proper communication. He will need to teach them the values of openness and enable them to experience some of the rewards of openness. Openness should not be indiscriminate; there are guidelines which should be followed. These guidelines are: (1) purpose (the objective of openness in any given situation); (2) manner (the method to be used to accomplish the purpose); and (3) timing (the appropriate time to engage in openness regarding the issue). When openness is governed by these three criteria it will result in a stronger, more satisfying relationship.

METHOD OF PROCEDURE

When both partners in a marriage desire to engage in counseling the pastor has several options open to him regarding procedure: (1) he can see both together; (2) he can see them individually; or (3) he can use a combination of the two. There are some situations which make separate interviews necessary, but there is much to commend the approach of the combination method. A typical marriage-counseling case involving, say, six sessions for each partner could be as follows: the first and last sessions the pastor would see the couple together; in sessions two through five he would see each partner separately. This approach enables him to see (in the first session) how the crisis is affecting each, how they relate and react to each other, who is more dominant and who is more passive, who is able to communicate better and who is able to hear better.

As he sees the partners separately, the pastor compiles new data which he analyzes in the light of the first joint session. As counseling continues, the pastor becomes more active in the process by giving information, sharing insights, offering suggestions, and evaluating the progress of each partner.

When the couple is seen together in the last session, the pastor is able to judge the gains that have been made as well as note the weak areas that still need attention. He will reinforce the gains and offer guidance in the areas that need to be strengthened. Seeing them together in the last session also gives him the opportunity of seeing how they are relating and communicating.

The process of marital counseling becomes greatly complicated if the pastor is able to see only one partner. (Sometimes one partner will refuse to enter counseling.) In such a situation the pastor does not get the full picture of the marital problem because he is viewing only one side of it. He will need to be aware that the counseling partner will unconsciously, if not consciously, present a somewhat distorted view of what is happening in the marriage. The pastor should also make it clear to the counseling partner that, under the circumstances, he will need to be willing to make even greater efforts to effect change than he would otherwise.

Sometimes a recalcitrant partner will change his mind

regarding entering counseling if he sees that his partner is in earnest about making the marriage better. This is especially so when he sees some changes in attitude and behavior taking place in the other mate. Sometimes an unwilling mate can be encouraged by the pastor to engage in the counseling process. A personal visit or a telephone call may be all that is needed to help him see his need for such help. If the pastor presents himself to the partner as an interested friend and not as an authority figure, he will most likely get the cooperation he seeks. However, the pastor should approach the matter in such a manner that the partner will find it easy to either accept or reject the offer of his services.

Conclusion

Some marital problems are like an inflamed appendix, capable of killing but relatively simple to remove. Other problems will be of such depth and severity that the pastor will not be able to deal with them. This means that he will need to refer them to a professional counselor, a psychologist or a psychiatrist. The pastor need not feel defeated by his inability to help such persons. If it is any comfort to him, he should be aware that some marital problems lie beyond the skill of even the best of professionals. Therefore, while he may be truly sorry that he is not able to help in some cases, he should not be embarrassed by this inability. Such failures should, however, encourage him to continue his study of counseling so that his knowledge will expand and his skills will increase.

9

Counseling Youth

Counseling with teen-agers does not require the application of a special set of techniques; rather, it requires the acquisition of a special set of understandings. The difference is at the point of knowledge, not skills. Before a pastor can help teen-agers he must understand them. This knowledge centers in the nature and characteristics of adolescence. The sequence regarding counseling with youth is: (1) understanding them, (2) relating to them, and (3) helping them.

Problems of Youth

There are some major problems that face the adolescent as he makes the transition from immaturity to maturity—some of them peculiar to this day. The pastor must have an understanding of these problems. Some of the major issues facing young people as they move from childhood to adulthood are as follows:

1. *Gaining independence from the home.* Emancipation from the home is hard on both parents and teen-agers. To one degree or another every youth is struggling for independence. This is what he wants more than anything else and he will pay almost any kind of price in order to gain it. However, he does not move in a steady progression toward independence. In fact, the youth who may on one occasion be extremely independent may suddenly regress to a very dependent mode of behavior.

A youth wants to be treated as an adult even if he is not behaving as an adult. Sometimes young people will assume unreasonable attitudes and engage in unreasonable behavior in order to affirm their independence. In short, they may assume a rebellious attitude. Usually rebellion serves two purposes: (1) to convince the adult world that the youth is independent; (2) to convince the youth himself that he is independent. A young person will test the limits of authority. He will consciously and unconsciously try to set the boundary lines within which he must live.

The interesting thing about this matter is that young people respect the authority they resent. While most young people do not like to live under authority, they feel insecure if the authority is not there. A college freshman, who was one of a family of 13 children, expressed to his counselor his frustration at not having to measure up to parental standards. He told his counselor that there were no limits set by his parents. The children could do what they wanted, go where they wanted, and observe the hours that they wanted. This left him with a great sense of insecurity, and he confessed that he envied his friends whose parents set limits on their behavior. He said, "If only they had said no to me!" Oddly enough, however, this same youth who wanted that kind of authority would have resented and resisted it had it been there.

The pastor should learn to trust young people. If he does

not truly trust them, this sense of distrust will somehow get through to them and they will realize that he views them as children, not as adults. He will find that it is wiser to talk things over with young people rather than tell them. Talking with them makes them feel like adults; telling them makes them feel like children.

The struggle for independence is a crisis through which young people pass and it is a struggle with which they have to deal. This means that their moods are likely to change quickly and drastically. The pastor who wants to relate to a youth will need to understand his moods, accept them, and not be unduly bothered by them.

2. *Gaining status in the group.* Acceptance by his peers is more important to a youth than acceptance by any other age-group. To the adolescent, only one group really matters— his associates. Sometimes this dismays parents, teachers, church workers, and pastors. So greatly concerned is the youth for the approval of his peers that he will seek to do everything that he can to be accepted by them. He will talk as they talk, dress as they dress, and act as they act. The young person constantly feels the need for social approval, and he will strive for it. If he does not get it, he may reject the group because he feels it has rejected him. When he leaves the group he may take one of several stances: (1) he may withdraw from all social relationships; (2) he may assume a "don't care" attitude; or (3) he may engage in over-aggressive behavior.

Being accepted by the group has some distinct benefits. It gives the young person security, a sense of belonging. It helps him to develop social skills. It gives him a refuge from the adult world, which he often views as oppressive, unfair, and hostile. Sometimes it will be the role of the pastor to help young persons learn social skills, so they can have the satisfaction of being accepted by their group. Sometimes he can help young people overcome characteristics which are disliked by the group. Further, if a pastor is aware of how important the group is to his young people, he will make very effort to develop a caring climate in the youth group of his church. A caring climate will draw new persons into the fellowship of the group and sustain those who are already in it. The pastor or youth leader will discourage cliques from developing. He will build a strong youth group that will become the most important peer group to each youth in his church.

3. *Using leisure time.* Young people sometimes have more time than they need or can use wisely, especially in the summer. They will need to be shown the value of engaging in hobbies, of participating in appropriate recreation activities, of developing new interests, and of using their time in service to God and the church. If young people remain inactive, boredom results. This gives opportunity for the improper use of time and it opens the door for them to engage in questionable conduct. If the church insists that youth refrain from such conduct—and it must—it means that it must also assume the obligation of helping provide suitable substitutes and attractive alternatives for their young people.

There are some implications that arise out of this: (1) the church must provide suitable recreational opportunities under the guidance of interested and dedicated youth workers; and (2) it must also provide opportunity for Christian service by its young people. Young people can engage in calling, canvassing, literature distribution, and work with the VBS. They can also become involved in work projects at the church. The church must view these activities by young persons as a ministry, not as busywork. The goal is not simply to keep young people out of trouble; it is also to help them to be a part of a ministry of the Church of Jesus Christ. The church must also encourage youth involvement in the summer camp programs, retreats, and institutes.

4. *Gaining financial independence.* It is not easy for some young people to make the transition from receiver to earner. Some persons never quite make that transition. However, most want to, and eventually do gain financial independence, but not before much conflict is experienced by both

young people and their parents. The financial independence that young people gain comes much later than most parents wish. Gaining financial independence is greatly affected by one's goals. A youth who has never shown much interest in work can suddenly become quite willing to work if he has a goal in mind, such as wanting to date, wanting to buy a car, wanting to save for his education, or wanting to get married.

5. *Selecting a vocation.* Selecting a vocation is a long-range goal which youth may need help in attaining. They are forced to think about their future vocation because of adult pressures, primarily from the home and the school. The desire for emancipation from the home demands that they think in terms of equipping themselves for a vocation. Also, a desire for marriage makes it mandatory to think in those terms.

The choice of a vocation is an overwhelming decision. What work shall I do? How will I like it? How much will I be paid? Will I advance? Is it important? Will it be fulfilling? What is God's will for my life? All of these questions, plus many more, create a kind of identity-crisis for the young person, for he cannot think in terms of his vocational future without thinking in terms of his self-concept. As he surveys the many alternatives theoretically open to him, he must realistically assess his own talents and abilities to determine if some of these alternatives are automatically closed to him. This creates a great crisis for young persons. In the process of finally arriving at a choice of vocation they will have made many tentative decisions.

The pastor must help his young people to see that even though they may not be called to be ministers, missionaries, and Christian education workers, still God has a claim on their lives and that they should view their choice of vocation in terms of what is God's will for them.

6. *Preparing for marriage.* Adolescence is the period when the youth develops his heterosexual interests. Puberty comes earlier for girls than boys, and girls also mature faster socially than boys. At this time (puberty), great interest is

shown in the opposite sex by both sexes. They want to be with each other but they do not know how to relate to each other. Adolescence is therefore a training ground for heterosexual relationships and it is a period of preparation for marriage. As the boy-girl interests are being developed, young people engage in many "loves." This means that they experience many joys and many hurts.

The church needs to be aware of the great transition through which young people are passing during the time of adolescence. It can make a tremendous contribution to young people and parents by creating sound family-life education programs. The church needs to teach young people a Christian view of sex which will round out the picture of biological sex that they are receiving through public education. The church also needs to do everything it can to build strong Christian homes, so that the young people can see a demonstration of what it means to live together in true love under the lordship of Christ.

7. *Arriving at a philosophy of life.* A philosophy of life has to do with the major values a youth acquires. These become the center around which his life will revolve. To change the figure, a philosophy of life becomes the frame into which he places the picture of his life. To this great issue the church can speak, and to it the church must speak. The church must challenge young people to become truly Christian in attitudes and responses as well as in personal religious experience. It has the task of revealing to young people the reality of God, of His desire to work in them, of His plans for them, and of the claims of Christ upon them.

CHARACTERISTICS OF ADOLESCENTS

1. *They are sensitive.* This may be for various reasons, many of them related to physical characteristics such as facial blemishes, caused by change in body chemistry; awkwardness, caused by more rapid growth than the muscles have

learned to accommodate, and by underdevelopment or over-development of the body. Through the mass media youth receives the culture's concept of the ideal body, with which he compares his own body. The difference between the ideal and the real is devastating for many young people and it causes them to be extremely sensitive.

Young people are also sensitive because they know that their interpersonal skills are lacking. Their peers, especially those of the opposite sex, are most important to them but they are uncertain what to do in order to gain peer approval.

Young people are also sensitive because they lack in self-understanding. Not only are they a puzzle to adults; they are also a puzzle to themselves. Changes in body, emotions, and thoughts are taking place so rapidly that they find they are living with a self they no longer know.

All of this means that young people are often difficult to understand and it is difficult to know how to relate to them.

2. *They are impulsive.* Young people are experiencing great emotional changes as well as great physical changes. They tend to approach life emotionally rather than rationally. This means that their behavior is likely to be erratic and unpredictable because they overreact to the immediate. Their uncertainty tends to make them jump to conclusions. They are not certain what they believe, but whatever they believe in at the moment, they believe in very strongly. A belief firmly held one day, however, may be discarded the next in favor of another of which they are equally sure.

3. *They are idealistic.* Their idealism causes them to wish for a perfect world, a perfect government, a perfect school, a perfect church, and a perfect home, all of these being directed by perfect authority figures. In short, young people wish for a perfect life and perfect people. Anything less than perfection is classified as "phony." Teen-agers reject what is, or appears to be, a fake. Disillusioned by the real, they often engage in fantasy which becomes more acceptable to their sense of idealism.

4. *They are insecure.* Because a teen-ager does not know why he feels as he does and why he behaves as he does, he experiences an enormous amount of insecurity. His search for personal identity has been unsuccessful; thus the boundaries of his being are blurred. In short, he does not know who he is. This is anxiety-producing and it makes him feel most insecure. He may wear many masks to hide his insecurity, such as conceit, brashness, daring, over-aggressiveness, withdrawal, and unconcern, but behind the mask is a scared soul in search for a self.

George Lawton has captured the adolescent attitude and expressed the adolescent hope in the following guidelines:

1.   Stand by us, not over us.
2.   Make us feel we are loved and wanted.
3.   Train us by being affectionately firm.
4.   Bring us up so we will not always need you.
5.   Try to be as consistent as possible.
6.   Don't try to make us feel inferior.
7.   Say, "Nice work," when we do something really well.
8.   Show respect for our wishes even if you disagree with them.
9.   Give direct answers to direct questions.
10.   Show interest in what we're doing.
11.   Treat us as if we are normal, even when our conduct seems peculiar to you.
12.   Teach us by example.
13.   Treat each one of us as a person in his own right.
14.   Don't keep us young too long.
15.   We need fun and companionship.
16.   Make us feel our home belongs to us.
17.   Don't laugh at us when we use the word "love."
18.   Treat us as a junior partner in the firm.
19.   Make yourself an adult fit for a child to live with.
20.   Prepare us to lead *our* lives, not *yours.*
21.   Give us the right to a major voice in our lives.
22.   Let us make our own mistakes.

23. Permit us the failings of average children—just as we permit you the failings of average parents.

If a pastor understands the problems youth are confronting as well as the characteristics of the adolescent personality, he will have bases for understanding and relating to them which he would not have otherwise. The pastor who wishes to give adequate guidance to the youth in his church should seek to learn more about adolescence in general and more about his young people in particular. He will seek to keep himself and his church in touch with young people's needs. He will not assume a condescending attitude toward them. He will often laugh with them but never laugh at them. He will seek to provide a leadership model, both in himself and in lay youth workers, which will evoke the respect and emulation of his youth. He will view young people as a vital segment of his church, seeking to bring them to a personal relationship with Christ. He will harness the energy and resources of his young people in fulfilling the mission of the church.

Following are some hypotheses which merit the serious consideration of the pastor who wishes to understand and relate to his young people:

Hypothesis No. 1: Youth, in every socioeconomic situation, are much more serious about their quest for a faith than we may have assumed.

Hypothesis No. 2: Ministering to others, the life and work of service, is much more highly valued by youth than we have supposed.

Hypothesis No. 3: New and more flexible forms and settings of youth ministry are needed in our highly mobile and fluid society.

Hypothesis No. 4: There is much more interest on the part of youth in communication and cooperation between youth and adults (including parents) than has been thought.

Hypothesis No. 5: While youth are the church in mission, they have special needs which the church must not overlook. [1]

As was said at the beginning of this chapter, counseling with teen-agers does not require the application of a special set of techniques. It necessitates the acquisition of a deeper understanding of the nature of adolescence. If a pastor exhibits such an understanding, his youth will sense it, appreciate it, and come to him for guidance and counseling.

The pastor who understands his young people will be afforded the challenge and responsibility of aiding them in making what has been called the three great decisions of youth—a mission, a mate, and a Master: something to do, someone to love, and Someone to serve.

10

Principles and Practices of Referral

It is not possible for a pastor to know answers to all of the problems that are presented to him in the course of his pastoral ministry. Happy is the pastor who recognizes this and is not embarrassed by his lack of understanding, for the range of dilemmas in which his people find themselves is wide indeed. The pastor who can accept his limitations without being defeated by them is a mature person who is released from the awesome task of trying to be somebody he is not. The mature pastor can admit to a person that he does not have the answer to his problem without a feeling of shame or inferiority.

While a pastor is not expected to have all of the answers to human problems, he is expected to know how to help his people find solutions to their problems. This is done through referral. Referral is the process of providing parishioners with information regarding where to find help and aiding them in receiving it. In every community there are resources available which can be of great assistance to persons in need.

Some of the persons to whom referrals can be made are medical doctors, lawyers, counselors, psychologists, psychiatrists, and social workers. Each of these is an expert in his field and his knowledge and skill should be utilized when needed. Other resources are city, county, and state welfare agencies, social service agencies, clinics and hospitals. The pastor should know the city, county, regional, and state resources that are available to his people, so that their services can be utilized when they are needed.

Early in any pastorate he assumes, the minister should make an inventory of the available referral resources, so that he can make intelligent referrals when they are necessary.

In most cases the matter of making referrals is fairly simple inasmuch as the problems of parishioners, outside of religious ones, will fall clearly in the province of another professional person such as a medical doctor or a lawyer. However this is not so regarding psychiatric referral because of the complex nature of mental illness. Because this is such a difficult decision which carries many deep implications, this matter will be given special and careful attention.

PSYCHIATRIC REFERRAL

The following is a representative descriptive definition of psychiatric referral by pastors which would generally be accepted by writers in the pastoral counseling field:

> [Referral] should be the church calling in specialized help in its ministry to the person as a whole. It naturally follows that in the process of therapy . . . the role of religion as a positive force becomes intensely relevant as the minister and the church take their place in vital relation to the psychiatrist and the hospital respectively.[1]

This definition of referral views the person as a whole,

acknowledges that the pastor is incapable of aiding the person alone, that the psychiatrist becomes the ally of the church, and that the pastor-parishioner relationship continues during and following psychiatric treatment. This definition of referral should be kept in mind as this discussion continues.

Without question, the pastor is in a key role in relation to the matter of mental illness. The question is not *if* he has a role in this problem; rather, it is a matter of how well he will perform it. The pastor, by the very nature of his role, is thrust into the major life situations of many of his parishioners—at birth, marriage, death, as well as at other crucial times. This also includes the crisis of mental illness which confronts many people today.

Laycock says that the clergyman may have a role to play in helping the mentally ill person to accept the need for treatment, trust the authorities to whom he is being admitted, and understand something of the nature of the treatment provided.[2] Many times the pastor functions as a counselor to the relatives of a mentally ill person rather than to the prospective patient himself. When this is so, the pastor's counseling becomes information-giving in nature. Laycock suggests that in this case the relatives will need help in realizing the following:

> (a) that mental illness is an illness like any other, and that it affects more people than polio, heart disease, and cancer combined; (b) that mental disease is not a single disease, and that it takes many forms; (c) that mental illness is not necessarily inherited—that constitutional factors of mental illness are not too well-known; (d) that mental illness does not attack without warning—that, while it may be precipitated by a crisis such as financial reverse or the loss of a loved one, this is merely the trigger on a gun already cocked; (e) that mental illness is treatable, and that the discharge rate from mental hospitals has been rapidly rising with the newer methods of treatment; and (f) that mental illness is no more a disgrace to the individual and his family than is the case of a family member's being ill with pneumonia, a heart condition, or cancer.[3]

Clinebell says:

> In relation to the psychotic person, his [the minister's]
> role is to *(a)* recognize the difficulty as mental illness;
> *(b)* aid the person in finding psychiatric help; *(c)* maintain
> a supportive pastoral relationship during treatment,
> whether the person is hospitalized or treated on an out-
> patient basis; *(d)* maintain a close relationship and be avail-
> able for counseling during the adjustment period following
> treatment.[4]

He says that, since many people trust his judgment and turn
to him spontaneously when trouble strikes, a pastor is in a
strategic position to assist them in finding competent, spe-
cialized help. He added, "A wise referral is one of the most
significant services he can render a suffering parishioner."

Whether a minister is dealing with a prospective patient
who is mentally ill or with the family of that person, the
nagging problem facing him is that of knowing *when* to refer
for psychiatric help. Obviously, if the person has lost contact
with reality, is a menace to himself, or is a threat to others, the
decision to refer is simple.[5] However, there are many times
when the matter of mental illness is not that deep-seated. It is
in regard to the latter that the minister must work through to
a decision regarding referral. Laycock says that this decision
will depend on five things: *(a)* the degree of general training
of the clergyman in the technique of counseling; *(b)* the kind
and quality of special training the clergyman has had for
dealing with this specific area of counseling; *(c)* the nature
of the problem; *(d)* the seriousness of the problem; *(e)* the
resources available to the parishioner. Laycock affirms that
the ultimate criterion must always be the highest welfare of
the patient.[6]

But this advice is not easy to follow for at least two reasons: (1) a given minister may not be equipped by professional training to make an adequate evaluation as to what the
"highest welfare" of the patient is; and (2) the minister is

often confused by the multitudinous warnings of the "experts" that he stay clear of psychiatric diagnosis.

Studies have shown clearly that most pastors' training has not equipped them to be at ease in dealing with deep-seated psychological problems in counseling. Blizzard carefully analyzed 80 seminaries' training programs and weighed these against their graduates' counseling experiences. He found that most of these men were not equipped to function adequately in the area of human relationships. His conclusion was that more and better training was needed in "behavioral" areas.[7] A study at the University of Denver revealed that mental health problems were the problems that ministers felt least equipped to handle.[8] A study by the Harvard University Project on Religion and Mental Health, in studying 100 Boston ministers, found that (1) only 10 percent of problems brought to the ministers pertained to religious questions; (2) psychological distress problems were second only to marriage and family problems in terms of frequency; and (3) the ministers felt least equipped to deal with psychological distress problems.[9]

Complicating the problem is that pastoral counseling literature abounds with strong cautions that pastors refrain from making psychiatric diagnoses and attempting psychiatric treatment.

The following are some of these representative warnings:

[The minister is not] to determine whether a person is mentally ill; that is a medical responsibility.[10]

A word of warning is in order for all those who are called upon to counsel troubled people. The determination of mental illness is the province of the psychiatrist.[11]

Except in the case of mild personality disorders, the clergyman should be anxious to help his parishioners to get such expert help as they require. He should be aware of his own limitations and avoid getting involved with psychiatric diagnosis and treatment.[12]

The minister should not attempt to diagnose the specific nature of the difficulty. This is the psychiatrist's area of competence and responsibility.[13]

Some clergymen have been known to discourage their parishioners from seeking needed psychiatric help. All depressed persons are potentially suicidal. By neglecting treatment [by a psychiatrist] a clergyman might be indirectly responsible for a tragedy which might be avoided.[14]

It becomes obvious as one reads pastoral counseling literature that the minister is to have no real stake in dealing with the mental illness himself. Such a study shows that the minister is instructed along the lines of "what to do until the psychiatrist arrives," rather than to aid him in dealing personally with a disturbed person. Mowrer feels that this is a most unfortunate situation and he believes that it reflects "one way in which the church has tried to make peace with the healing professions."[15] He questions whether this "division of labor" corresponds to reality. He also questions the labeling of mental illness as sickness, rather than sin.[16] He says:

At the very time that psychologists are becoming distrustful of the sickness approach to personality disturbance and are beginning to look with more benign interest and respect toward certain moral and religious precepts, religionists themselves are being caught up in and bedazzled by the same preposterous system of thought as that from which we psychologists are just recovering.[17]

Mowrer believes that the biochemical explanation for mental illness is an attempt to keep it in the exclusive domain of medicine; therefore the clergy would be excused from this responsibility.[18] He also believes that because they have been continually reminded of their "limitations" they lack the confidence to deal with mental illness problems.[19]

Regardless of this concept of the role of the pastor in relation to mental illness, it must be remembered that, comparatively speaking, Mowrer is the "voice of *one* crying in the wilderness"; that the preponderance of advice to ministers is that they refrain from attempting treatment of the mentally ill.

The fact that pastors are ill at ease in psychological-distress situations, along with the above-mentioned "cautions" in ministers' counseling literature, could cause many of them to make psychiatric referrals when such referrals may not be needed. The minister who facilitates an unnecessary referral needs to be aware of certain end results that could arise out of such a referral.

Some Considerations Affecting Psychiatric Referral

1. *Decision to refer may be based primarily upon others evaluations of mental illness.* Mechanic says that there are differing definitions of mental illness that are made in varying locations in the social structure.[20] For example, the patient may define his own illness in terms of how he feels; his employer might judge him as being ill because he deviates from group requirements; and his family may consider him ill on the basis of the attitude he professes or his situational be-behavior.

Because there is no universally accepted definition of mental illness, it is quite possible that a minister may be unduly influenced by others' views of mental illness. If he accepts and acts upon the evaluations of others, he may be lending his "significant other" influence that will facilitate a person's future treatment or hospitalization whether he needs it or not. This is not to say that a pastor may be ignorant of the manifestations of mental illness; rather, inasmuch as he is often not permitted to fully view the behavior of a prospective patient, he may, unfortunately, make his decision to refer on the basis of what is reported to him, not on the basis of how the person is actually behaving.

Such referral may facilitate a family's disposition of an unwanted person who may not actually be mentally ill. Let us assume that a minister will always value the dignity of human personality. This being so, he could not conscientiously contribute to a process that could militate against the dignity and rights of an individual. However, if he bases his decision to refer primarily, if not exclusively, on the evaluation of others, he may well be working against the best interests of the individual in question.

The minister must not assume that his, or others', evaluations of mental illness are not crucial ones. Mechanic says:

> The layman usually assumes that his conception of mental illness is not the important definition since the psychiatrist is the expert and presumably makes the final decision. On the contrary, community persons are brought to the hospital on the basis of lay definitions, and once they arrive, their appearance alone is usually regarded as sufficient evidence of illness. [21]

Such referral may set in motion a process that is both unnecessary and undesirable. Mechanic further states that the basic decision about mental illness is usually made by the community members and not professional persons, and that the psychiatrist who practices in large treatment centers must often *assume* the illness of the patient. He says that, while the persons who are obviously ill are usually found in mental hospitals, there are some persons who are just as ill who go unattended while moderately sick people receive treatment. "This selection," he says, "is clearly based on social criteria, not on psychiatric ones." [23] If Mechanic is correct in his analysis, it is obvious that a minister could very conceivably be an unsuspecting party to initiating treatment for persons who may not need it.

2. *Referral may be tantamount to hospitalization whether a person is mentally ill or not.* Mechanic studied two mental hospitals for a period of three months and he reported that he never observed a case where the psychiatrist advised the patient that he did not need treatment. Rather, all who appeared at the hospital were drawn into the patient population. [24] It cannot be assumed that what Mechanic found would be universally true, but the evidence is too weighty to

assume that it does not happen often. The minister must realize, then, that, by referral, he may actually be prescribing hospitalization when he is merely attempting to aid a person in obtaining a professional diagnosis. Thus his "layman's" opinion may become, in effect, a professional diagnosis.

Wiesbauer, in characterizing the proper attitude of the pastor regarding hospitalization of a mentally ill person, says, "His function is the difficult one of a compassionate neutral."[25] One wonders what really is the extent of this neutrality.

3. *Referral may result in crippling an individual vocationally after he is "cured" of his mental illness.* Vocational placement often becomes quite difficult if the employer is aware of the applicant's past mental illness. Olshansky, Grob, and Malamud found that employers prefer not to hire known ex-mental patients. They say, "Further evidence of that preference is that only five employers interviewed expressed a willingness to consider hiring any qualified ex-mental patients in the immediate future."[26] These employers objected mainly for these reasons: (1) fear of violence, (2) fear that such employees would be "incompatible," and (3) fear of bizarre behavior.

It was further found that the employers tended to believe that ex-mental patients could be suitable only for certain types of unskilled jobs because they were not "pressure" jobs, "responsible" jobs, "hazardous" jobs, or "difficult" jobs. The ex-mental patient is clearly viewed as a risk by employers. The minister contemplating psychiatric referral should keep this fact in mind. If his referral is not justified, he may contribute to a process that could make the patient's prospect of finding employment difficult or, in some cases, force the patient to do a lower level of work than he is qualified to do. This is in keeping with Scheff's proposition that "labeled deviants are punished when they attempt to return to conventional roles."[27] Robert C. Hunt, M. D., of the Hudson River State Hospital, Poughkeepsie, N.Y., says:

> The man who recovers from an attack of mental illness
> with his vocational skills intact and is then refused employ-
> ment is just as disabled, vocationally, as though his intrinsic
> capacity for work had been totally destroyed. [28]

Linn and Schwarz cautioned against what they called
"premature referral." In reporting a study by the Department
of Health at Yale University they said that there was wide-
spread fear of psychiatrists among the student body. It was
felt that this was due partly to the labeling process that would
disqualify them for vocational positions irrespective of their
abilities. They concluded that many students who needed,
even wanted, psychiatric help avoided it. [29]

4. *Referral may result in disrupting the normal ongoing
processes of a person's life in terms of the fact of hospitalization.* It is not unusual for hospitalization for the mentally ill
to extend over a period of many years. It is granted that some,
maybe many, persons need to be hospitalized for great periods
of time, but one wonders if this is necessary for all such persons who are presently in mental hospitals. There is research
evidence to support the fact that there is a correlation between economic level and length of hospitalization. White, in
citing the well-known Hollingshead and Redlich study, says:

> . . . 93% of low-income patients in state hospitals were
> still incarcerated ten years after admission. Psychiatrists
> wonder why the poor resist psychotherapy, and attribute
> their resistance to ignorance or bias. In plain fact, low-
> income people see that mental illness leads to mental hos-
> pitals, one of the worst catastrophes that can befall any
> man. [30]

Hollingshead and Redlich noted an astonishing class differen-
tial in psychiatric diagnosis and treatment. They discovered
that what is called a neurosis if you have money is called a
psychosis if you have none, and that the well-to-do are treated
with individual or group psychotherapy, while the poor are
hospitalized.

5. *Referral may result in expensive psychiatric treat-*

ment which may be beyond the economic reach of many persons. If there were ample evidence to believe that such expense resulted in definite cures for the mentally ill, the cost could be easily justified. However, it is well-known that psychiatric treatment may be both lengthy and costly and that often little benefit is derived. Much of the promised "success" of psychiatric treatment is predicated on the necessity for long-term relationships. Persons with limited means often fail to continue treatment because they do not see quick results and so terminate treatment prematurely. This tends to prejudice them against psychiatry and thus excludes them from receiving the benefits that could have resulted from treatment of a longer duration.

6. *Referral may result in initiating a treatment program from which little benefit may be derived.* As Mowrer has observed, the results of psychiatric treatment are far from flattering to psychiatry. He suggests that not only are the "cures" in limited number but also that even some psychiatrists freely admit their lack of success.[31]

7. *Referral may result in a person's being stigmatized as a result of psychiatric treatment.* There is a sharp difference between what the literature says society's attitude should be toward the mentally ill and how society actually views the mentally ill. Though society should not view mental illness as a disgrace to the individual or to his family, the fact remains that that is precisely what society does. As Biddle says, "Those who have suffered mental illness have committed no crime, but how often society snubs them on return to community life!"[32] Goffman, in his book *Stigma: Notes on the Management of Spoiled Identity*, deals at length with the matter of the stigma attached to the mentally ill. He characterizes this as "the situation of the individual who is disqualified for social acceptance."[33] Thus, every person who is labeled as mentally ill runs the risk of being stigmatized by his fellows. This complicates his problem in that the last thing such a person needs is to feel that he is unwanted and unaccepted.

The minister should exercise extreme caution so that he will not make an unnecessary referral that could result in a parishioner's facing the debilitating effects of social stigma.

8. *Psychiatric referral may result in a patient's being dislodged from his religious orientation.* Some psychiatrists, particularly of the Freudian school, are not only anti-religion; they identify religion as part of the patient's problem. If a psychiatrist seriously believes this to be true, he would conceive it to be his "duty" to divest his patient of his "religion neurosis" in order to effect a personality cure. Fairbanks says that a psychiatrist rarely "returns" a parishioner-patient to the referring minister. In fact, it is an interesting phenomenon that many hospitals and many physicians try to shield their patients from the minister and religion.[34] To a person with a religious orientation, this denial of the validity of religion could be devastating.

When Referrals Should Be Made

Referrals should be made to other professional persons or agencies under the following circumstances:

1. When it is clearly evident that the parishioner's problem is beyond the scope of the pastor's ability to help.

2. When there are competent persons in the community or area who are qualified to help.

3. When the pastor can make such referrals in clear conscience that his parishioner's faith will not be destroyed nor his future social relationships jeopardized.

4. When he can turn loose of the problem but hold on to the parishioner in a supportive relationship.

Guidelines for Making Referrals

1. Know the professional person or agency best qualified to help a parishioner with a particular problem.

2. Have confidence in the competency and integrity of the referral source.

121

3. Support the professional person or agency in the course being pursued toward solution of the parishioner's problem unless there is clear evidence that it is not benefiting him.

4. Refuse to offer counsel regarding a problem that is being dealt with by another professional person or agency.

5. Continue a supportive relationship with a parishioner during and following referral.

Reference Notes

CHAPTER 1

1. Seward Hiltner, *Religion and Mental Health* (New York: The Macmillan Co., 1943), p. 173.

2. William E. Hulme, *How to Start Counseling* (New York: McGraw-Hill Book Company, Inc., 1945), p. 14.

3. Murray H. Leiffer, *In That Case . . .* (Chicago: Willett, Clark and Company, 1938), pp. 1-2.

4. Russell L. Dicks, *Pastoral Work and Personal Counseling* (New York: The Macmillan Company, 1949), p. 7.

5. Thomas Holman, "The Church's Work with Individuals," *The Church at Work in the Modern World*, William Clayton Bower, ed. (Chicago: The University of Chicago Press, 1935), p. 134.

6. Leland Foster Wood, "The Training of Ministers for Marriage and Family Counseling," *Marriage and Family Living* 12, No. 2 (spring, 1950), 46.

7. John Sutherland Bonnell, *Psychology for Pastor and People* (New York: Harper and Brothers, 1948), p. 173.

8. Sidney E. Goldstein, *Marriage and Family Counseling* (New York: McGraw-Hill Book Co., Inc., 1945), p. 14.

9. Hulme, *op. cit.*, p. 14.

10. Carroll A. Wise, *Pastoral Counseling, Its Theory and Practice* (New York: Harper and Brothers, 1951), p. 40.

11. *Ibid.*

11. John Sutherland Bonnell, *Pastoral Psychiatry* (New York: Harper and Brothers, 1938), p. 227.

13. *Ibid.*, p. 201.

14. Seward Hiltner, *The Counselor in Counseling* (New York: Abingdon-Cokesbury Press, 1952), p. 10.

15. Karl L. Stolz, *The Church and Psychotherapy* (New York: Abingdon-Cokesbury Press, 1943), p. 234.

16. Bonnell, *Pastoral Psychiatry*, p. 55.

17. Wise, *op. cit.*, p. 40.

18. Hiltner, *The Counselor in Counseling*, p. 7.

19. James J. Cribbin, *Catholic Educational Review* 53, No. 2 (Feb. 1955), 58.

CHAPTER 2

1. G. Bromley Oxnam, *The Ethical Ideals of Jesus in a Changing World* (New York: Abingdon-Cokesbury Press, 1941), p. 15.

2. *Ibid.*, p. 16.

3. Phillips Brooks, *The Influence of Jesus* (New York: E. P. Dutton and Co., 1880), p. 112.

4. Oxnam, *op. cit.*, p. 56.

5. Ernest F. Scott, *The Ethical Teaching of Jesus* (New York: The Macmillan Co., 1927), p. 58.

6. *Ibid.*, p. 83.

7. Emory S. Bogardus, *The Development of Social Thought*, (New York: Longmans, Green and Co., 1947), p. 150.

CHAPTER 4

1. J. H. Jowett, *The Preacher: His Life and Work* (New York: George H. Doran Co., 1912), p. 23.

2. Jack Gullege, "Preachers' Changing Image," *Arkansas Baptist*, Dec. 3, 1964.

3. William E. Hulme, *Your Pastor's Problems* (Garden City, N.J.: Doubleday and Co., 1968), p. 20.

4. Paul E. Johnson, *Person and Counselor* (Nashville: Abingdon Press, 1967), p. 30.

5. Oswald Sanders, *Spiritual Leadership* (Chicago: Moody Press, 1967), p. 70.

6. *Ibid.*, p. 25.

7. Samuel M. Shoemaker, *With the Holy Spirit and with Fire* (New York: Harper and Brothers, 1960), p. 88.

8. Howard J. Clinebell, *Basic Types of Pastoral Counseling* (Nashville: Abingdon Press, 1966), p. 15.

9. Alvin J. Lindgren, *Foundations for Purposeful Church Administration* (Nashville: Abingdon Press, 1965), p. 90.

10. Clinebell, *op. cit.*, p. 14.

11. Maxie D. Dunnam, Gary J. Herbertson, and Everett L. Shostrom, *The Manipulator and the Church* (Nashville: Abingdon Press, 1968), p. 91.

12. Edgar N. Jackson, *A Psychology for Preaching* (New York: Channel Press, Inc., 1961), p. 178.

CHAPTER 5

1. Wise, *op. cit.*, pp. 18-19.

2. Stolz, *op. cit.*, p. 11.

3. Wise, *op. cit.*, p. 11.

4. Rollo May, *The Art of Counseling* (New York: Abingdon-Cokesbury, 1939), p. 11.

5. Wise, *op. cit.*, p. 115.
6. *Ibid.*, p. 103.
7. Hiltner, *The Counselor in Counseling*, p. 133.
8. Bonnell, *Pastoral Psychiatry*, p. 227.
9. *Ibid.*, p. 55.

Chapter 6

1. Milton E. Hahn and Malcolm S. MacLean, *Counseling Psychology* (New York: McGraw-Hill Book Co., Inc., 1955), p. 81.
2. Quoted by Hahn and MacLean, *ibid.*
3. Clifford E. Erickson, *The Counseling Interview* (New York: Prentice-Hall, Inc., 1950), p. 57.
4. Everett L. Shostrom and Lawrence M. Brammer, *The Dynamics of the Counseling Process* (New York: McGraw-Hill Book Co., Inc., 1952), p. 126.
5. Erickson, *op. cit.*, pp. 8, 90.
6. *Ibid.*, p. 45.
7. Hahn and MacLean, *op. cit.*, p. 78.
8. Erickson, *op. cit.*, pp. 59-60.
9. Hahn and MacLean, *op. cit.*, p. 83.

Chapter 9

1. Marvin J. Taylor, *An Introduction to Christian Education* (New York: Abingdon Press, 1966), pp. 187-91.

Chapter 10

1. Wayne E. Oates, *Religious Factors in Mental Illness* (New York: Association Press, 1955), p. 155.
2. Samuel R. Laycock, *Pastoral Counseling for Mental Health* (New York: Abingdon Press, 1961), p. 59.
3. *Ibid.*
4. Howard J. Clinebell, Jr., *Mental Health Through the Christian Community* (New York: Abingdon Press, 1965), pp. 242-43.
5. Thomas W. Klink, "Clergymen's Guide in Recognizing Serious Mental Illness," pamphlet, The National Association for Mental Health, Inc. (not paginated).
6. Laycock, *op. cit.*, pp. 24-25.
7. Samuel W. Blizzard, "The Roles of the Rural Parish Minister, the Protestant Seminaries, and the Sciences of Social Behavior," *Religious Education*, Vol. 50, Nov.—Dec., 1955.
8. James D. Hamilton, "An Analysis of Professional Prepara-

tion for Pastoral Counseling" (unpublished doctoral dissertation, University of Denver, Denver, Colo., 1959).

9. Hans Hoffman, *The Ministry and Mental Health* (New York: Association Press, 1960), p. 225.

10. Klink, *op. cit.* (not paginated).

11. Ernest E. Bruder, *Ministering to Deeply Troubled Persons* (Englewood Cliffs, N.J.: Prentice-Hall, Inc., 1963), p. 26.

12. Laycock, *op. cit.*, p. 96.

13. Clinebell, *Mental Health Through the Christian Community*, p. 244.

14. W. E. Biddle, *Integration of Religion and Psychiatry* (New York: The Macmillan Co., 1955), p. 125.

15. O. H. Mowrer, *Crisis in Psychiatry and Religion* (Princeton, N.J.: D. Van Nostrand Co., 1961), p. 32.

16. *Ibid.*, p. 49.

17. *Ibid.*, p. 52.

18. *Ibid.*, p. 44.

19. *Ibid.*, p. 45.

20. David Mechanic, "Social Factors in Identifying and Defining Mental Illness," *Mental Hygiene*, Vol. 46, Jan., 1962.

21. *Ibid.*

22. *Ibid.*

23. *Ibid.*

24. *Ibid.*

25. Henry H. Wiesbauer, "Pastoral Help in Serious Mental Illness" (pamphlet, The National Association for Mental Health, Inc., not paginated).

26. Simon Olshansky, Samuel Grob, and Irene T. Malamud, "Employers' Attitudes and Practices in the Hiring of Ex-mental Patients," *Mental Hygiene*, Vol. 42, July, 1958.

27. Thomas Scheff, "The Role of the Mentally Ill and the Dynamics of Social Disorder," *Sociometry*, Vol. 26, December, 1963.

28. Olshansky, Grob, and Malamud, *op. cit.*

29. Lows Linn and Leo Schwarz, *Psychiatry and Religious Experience* (New York: Random House, 1958), p. 274.

30. Dale White, "Mental Health and the Poor," *Concern*, October 15, 1964.

31. Mowrer, *op. cit.*, pp. 76, 83, 121, 137.

32. Biddle, *op. cit.*, p. 150.

33. E. Goffman, *Stigma: Notes on the Management of Spoiled Identity* (Englewood Cliffs, N.J.: Prentice-Hall, 1963).

34. Rollin J. Fairbanks, "Cooperation Between Clergy and Psychiatrists," *Pastoral Psychology* 2, No. 16 (Sept., 1951), 211.